# CIVIC TOURISM
## *The Poetry and Politics of Place*

Four Community Conversations About Belonging *in* and *to* "Place."

As an Industry, as Residents, as Guests.

## Dan Shilling
### Foreword by Scott Russell Sanders

*Examine each question in terms of what is ethically and*

*esthetically right, as well as what is economically expedient.*

*A thing is right when it tends to preserve the integrity,*

*stability, and beauty of the biotic community.*

*It is wrong when it tends otherwise.*

~Aldo Leopold, "The Land Ethic"

# CIVIC TOURISM

## *Mission*

To reframe tourism's purpose, from an *end* to a *means*—that is, from a market-driven growth goal to a tool that can help the public preserve and enhance what they love about their place, while revitalizing the local economy.

## *Strategies*

1. *Rethink Economics* urges communities to connect tourism planning to restorative, place-based market policies.

2. *Connect to the Public* recommends engagement practices that foster understanding of and support for a responsible tourism ethic.

3. *Invest in the Story* encourages a robust conceptual and financial commitment to place-making.

Civic tourism is about appreciating tourism as a public good, valuing it as a public responsibility, and practicing it as a public art.

Inquiries regarding requests to reprint all or part of *Civic Tourism: The Poetry and Politics of Place* should be addressed to Sharlot Hall Museum Press.

Published by Sharlot Hall Museum Press
415 West Gurley Street
Prescott, Arizona 86301
928-445-3122
www.sharlot.org

First edition.

Design by Ericka Cero Wood, Cero Wood Graphic Design, Inc.


Printed in the United States of America.

This publication was made possible in part by a grant from
The Institute of Museum and Library Services.

All proceeds from the sale of this publication support public programs
at Sharlot Hall Museum and a scholarship fund at Arizona State University.

ISBN  978-0-927579-26-1

10 9 8 7 6 5 4 3 2

# CONTENTS

*for the place makers*

*It is obvious that one has to grant*

*priority to place.*

~Archytas

# THE GEOGRAPHY OF SOMEWHERE

## *Scott Russell Sanders*

Americans gad about too much. Our ceaseless mobility burns up the earth's dwindling supply of petroleum, destabilizes the climate, enslaves us to tyrannical regimes in the Middle East, embroils us in war, buries more and more of our landscape under pavement, and shatters our communities. No person concerned about the fate of our planet and the welfare of our descendants would encourage any more idle movement. What Dan Shilling proposes here is an antidote to such aimless wandering.

Travel at its best can be a kind of vision quest, in which we journey away from the familiar world to encounter some alien setting, some natural or cultural or spiritual presence that enlarges our understanding, and then we journey home to act out that larger vision in our households, neighborhoods, towns, and cities. As in a mythic quest, what begins as a private search ends up enhancing the life of the tribe. If that sounds like a grand comparison, well, it is meant to be grand, but also attainable and compelling.

Too often, however, the kind of travel we call tourism is only another form of shopping, treating the whole country as a gigantic mall offering trinkets and distractions for sale. Too often, it is driven by a yen for golfing or gambling, a craving for novelty or scenery, or by simple boredom. If we're going to rove about the continent, burning up oil and jeopardizing our grandchildren's future, we ought to be prompted by larger motives. Can tourism become something more meaningful and rewarding not only to travelers but also to the places they visit and the home places to which they return? I hope so; I believe so; and that is why I am offering these words of introduction to this pioneering book.

Why do so many American towns and cities feel like jumbles rather than communities, without pattern or purpose? What it means to lack a sense of place was memorably expressed by Gertrude Stein. On a return trip to the United States after years of living in Europe, Stein visited Oakland, California, where she had grown up. She could find no trace of her childhood home, no durable landmarks at all, leading her to remark that she could not imagine settling down and writing in Oakland, for "there is no there there."

Whether Stein's judgment was fair in the 1930s, when she voiced it, or whether it is fair now, I can't say, since I have never set foot in Oakland. But her judgment strikes me as all too true of many American cities and towns, where any sense of character or coherence has been eroded by the forces of development. Uniform highway design, strip malls, cookie-cutter suburbs, manufactured housing, garish franchise architecture, and box stores surrounded by deserts of blacktop have made our settlements less and less distinct from one another.

The mass media contribute to this homogenizing of America by smearing across the land a single, sleazy imagery whose overriding goal is to grab our attention and sell it to sponsors, and whose underlying goal may be to mold our minds into thinking as the owners of the media wish us to think. Chains of radio stations play the same music and recite the same headlines; chains of newspapers print the same articles; chains of bookstores feature the same books; cable and satellite networks beam the same programs from Florida to Alaska. Over the airwaves, on billboards and T-shirts, through computers and phones, the usual products are peddled coast to coast. As a result of these trends, we spend more and more of our lives in built environments or in virtual environments that are monotonous, ephemeral, rootless, and ugly.

If you happen to live in a place that has preserved its distinctive features, you may think I exaggerate. But for every idyllic New England village, for every Portland, Oregon, or pre-Katrina New Orleans, for every Santa Fe or Sitka, for every Beacon Hill or Greenwich Village or Chinatown there are hundreds of American places that have lost touch with their past, have cut themselves off from their surrounding landscape, have succumbed to the blight of sprawl. Even in the best-preserved places, the same corrosive influences are at work.

Every now and again, here and there, citizens will rise up and defend their turf against invasion by Wal-Mart, McDonald's, or some other Goliath; but Goliath never sleeps, never takes no for an answer, never runs out of money or political friends, and eventually the giant gets its way. So the homogenizing of America goes implacably on, street by street, real estate parcel by parcel, restaurant by office by store, and we adjust to this regimentation in the same way that we adjust to rising levels of pollution, congestion, violence, and noise. Over the past half century, we have surrendered to the tyranny of automobiles, as if their care and feeding were the central purpose of cities, and we have allowed our home places to become the colonies of global corporations, which bear no connection to local history, culture, or terrain. The resulting desolate hodgepodge is what James Howard Kunstler has called "The Geography of Nowhere."

One cannot feel delight or pride in a place, a sense of belonging to a place, or a concern for the well-being of a place, if "there is no there there." So it's not surprising that the erosion of our towns and cities has coincided with a retreat by Americans from civic life. The two trends reinforce one another. Our cityscapes and landscapes turn into jumbles because not enough people are looking after them, and ever fewer people are willing to look after places that have lost their souls.

The retreat from civic life has been documented by Robert Bellah and his colleagues in *Habits of the Heart* and *The Good Society*, by Daniel Kemmis in

*Community and the Politics of Place*, and by Robert Putnam in *Bowling Alone*, to mention a few examples of a growing literature. These authors observe that Americans are less and less able to talk about or even to acknowledge any rights or interests aside from those of the individual, and consequently we are becoming ever more reluctant to join together to seek pleasure or to serve our common needs. These trends coincide with the triumph of television, which purveys the solipsistic, hedonistic, ahistorical mindset we blithely call consumerism. The whole structure of modern life—solitary viewing of screens, isolation in cars or cubicles, advertising's emphasis on personal gratification—cuts us off from communal experiences and public concerns.

Whatever the reasons for this cultural shift, in recent decades increasing numbers of Americans have been withdrawing from involvement with local schools, clubs, and cultural institutions; giving up their subscriptions to local newspapers; abandoning main street merchants in favor of chain stores; neglecting to vote and otherwise ignoring community politics, except to demand lower taxes. The burgeoning megachurches may seem to be an exception to the solipsistic trend, but they are in fact another symptom of it, for they tend to focus on personal salvation rather than service to one's neighbor, on heavenly bliss rather than earthly renewal.

And as we retreat from civic life, where do we go? Into the frenzy of private consumption, which often necessitates longer working hours and second jobs; into therapy of one sort or another; into drink and drugs and other chemical pacifiers. Year by year, we spend less time outdoors interacting with neighbors or observing nature, more time in air-conditioned cars negotiating traffic or indoors transfixed by the electronic never-never land flickering on screens. Those screens tell us, through programs as well as advertising, that our pleasure, appearance, comfort, and status matter more than anything else; they tell us that the earth exists to satisfy our cravings; they tell us that we alone, out of all species and all generations, are the ones who count.

In the face of narcissism and homogenization, it is all the more vital that we recover a sense of place. A powerful sense of belonging to our home ground can draw us out of our self-preoccupation and revive our concern for the public realm. It can help transform us from rootless wanderers into inhabitants, from consumers into stewards. The kind of tourism that interests me, the only kind I am willing to advocate, would challenge and inspire travelers by providing them with experience of a real place, a distinctive place, a place with its own history, culture, and texture. This is what I imagine civic tourism to be—an immersion of the traveler in the geography of *some*where.

What are the qualities of a real place, a distinctive place, a place with its own history, culture, and texture? What qualities give certain places a feeling of character and charisma, makes them worthy of a visitor's deep engagement and of a citizen's love?

To begin with, a real place feels as though it belongs where it is, as though it has grown there, shaped by weather and geography, rather than being imported from elsewhere and set down arbitrarily like a mail-order kit. The connection to geography shows up in building materials, such as the adobe of Arizona and New Mexico, the cedar of Oregon, the limestone of Indiana, or the pine of Georgia and Maine; it shows up in architecture, such as the shady verandas of the Gulf Coast, the passageways linking house to barn in New England, the silos and grain elevators jutting from the prairie horizon of the Midwest, or the steel roofs on the rainy west flanks of the Cascade Mountains; and it shows up in food, such as Boston clam chowder or New Orleans gumbo or Milwaukee beer or Kansas City steak.

A real place is also distinguished by a vigorous local economy, one that draws on resources from the region and on the skills of its own citizens. Key enterprises, from factories to coffee shops, reflect the taste and judgment of the local people who own them, rather than the dictates of distant corporations. Although such an economy may produce goods and services for sale in the global market, it begins by serving the needs of the community, for jobs and healthcare as well as for food, shelter, clothing, and entertainment. Dollars spent in the community circulate there for a spell, instead of being immediately whisked away to some remote headquarters.

Visitors will know they have arrived in a real place when they deal with clerks who do not wear uniforms, when they find in shops well-crafted articles whose makers live nearby, when they discover on restaurant menus dishes they could not order anywhere else. They will know they have arrived in a cherished place when artists choose not merely to live there but to photograph and paint it, to write and sing of it; when archaeologists and historians delve into its past; when naturalists keep track of the local flora and fauna; and when elders pass on all of this lore to the young.

A real place also conveys a sense of temporal depth, a sense that people have been living and laboring here for a long time. The traces of earlier generations are preserved in festivals and folkways and habits of speech; in old buildings that have been restored and kept in service; in landscapes that are still devoted to orchards, dairies, woodlots and other traditional uses. While honoring the past, a real place is not trapped there, the way Colonial Williamsburg, Plymouth Plantation, Dearborn Village, and other historical reconstructions are frozen in time. A real place is alive and changing, like any organism, gaining and losing residents, tearing down and building up. Yet there is continuity amid the change. However shiny the new surface of a dynamic city or town, it does not obliterate the deeper layers. New construction harmonizes with earlier architecture. New practices acknowledge older customs. Newcomers learn from old-timers.

Although a place like Taos or Tucson is in danger of being smothered by the effects of its own charm, the charm endures, and it has much to do with the layered presence of Native American, Hispanic, and Anglo influence, a tumultuous history stretching back over centuries. In a nation still relatively new, reminders of the past are all the more precious. Visitors crowd the streets of Concord, Massachusetts, to commune with the ghosts of Thoreau, Emerson, Hawthorne, and other worthies. Visitors stroll the avenues of Oak Park, Illinois, to see among the recent houses a handful of lovingly preserved homes designed by Frank Lloyd Wright; they flock to Philadelphia to behold, in the midst of flashy newness, the Liberty Bell or the gravestone of Ben Franklin or an eighteenth-century Quaker meetinghouse; they journey to spots in Kentucky, Indiana, and Illinois to see traces of Lincoln, and they range from Gettysburg to Vicksburg in search of Civil War battlefields. Tokens of the past may be newly-built, such as the arch at St. Louis commemorating Lewis & Clark's journey of discovery, or the reconstructed boats in Green River, Utah, modeled after those used by John Wesley Powell on his descent of the Colorado. We glimpse a past reaching back more than a thousand years in the architecture and lifeways of Hopi pueblos or Tlingit villages, and we sense an even deeper past among the ancient earthworks of the Upper Mississippi and its tributaries, as at Cahokia in Illinois or the Serpent Mound in Ohio.

Even when the history is troubling—as it is in the massacre site at Wounded Knee or the slave market of Charleston or the whaling wharfs of New Bedford or the industrial ruins of Pittsburgh—we are better off knowing the history than ignoring it, and each of these places is more engrossing for having preserved a record of its past. The presence of history, good and bad, not only enriches our experience of place, it also reminds us that we who are alive now suffer as well as benefit from the actions of our ancestors, and that our actions, in turn, will affect those who come after us. Americans need such a reminder now more than ever, as we add hundreds of billions of dollars each year to the national debt our children will have to repay, as we use up natural resources at an accelerating rate, and as we degrade the biosphere.

A real place keeps us mindful of nature, as it keeps us mindful of history. In the built environment one feels the presence of the living environment—in parks, gardens, bike and pedestrian trails, river corridors, beaches, urban forests, and yards given over to native plants, and in all the creatures, from crows to coyotes, that share the place with our two-legged kind. Imagine New York City without Central Park, or Chicago without the lakefront, or Madison without the arboretum. One cannot think of Lexington, Kentucky, apart from the necklace of bluegrass horse farms, or of Moscow, Idaho, without the rolling doeskin hills of the Palouse, or Burlington without the shimmering border of Lake Champlain, or Denver without its view of the Rockies, or San Francisco without the Bay.

Although we can't summon up spectacular settings for our home places, we can make the most of whatever nature gives us. In recent years, Providence,

Rhode Island, has uncovered the rivers that flow through downtown; Louisville has restored the riverfront along the Ohio, Indianapolis has built a string of parks beside the White River, Cleveland has become reacquainted with Lake Erie; and in doing so, each city has reclaimed some of its identity. Even if our home grounds are not blessed with big rivers or great lakes, we can support land trusts and local governments in their efforts to expand the amount of green space in our communities; we can turn abandoned railway lines into trails and turn vacant lots into gardens; we can plant trees along our streets; we can replace our lawns with native shrubs and wildflowers and ferns; we can grow food for birds and butterflies as well as for ourselves; we can create ponds and prairies in our school grounds, enabling children to play safely in patches of wildness; we can limit sprawl, so that open country remains within reach of city dwellers; we can shade outdoor lights and clean up the air and welcome the stars back into our night skies.

A community can also maintain its link to the countryside by feeding itself at least partly from nearby sources—often through farmers' markets, where local produce is sold directly by growers to eaters, instead of being shipped hundreds or thousands of miles. If you were to visit my hometown of Bloomington, Indiana, depending on the season, you could walk with me among market stalls heaped with corn, fragrant cantaloupes, gourds the size of basketballs, eggplants like giant purple tears, and beeswax candles smelling of meadows. You could gather the whole alphabet of fruits and vegetables, from apples to zucchinis, or a bouquet of gladiolas, poppies, lotus blossoms, and phlox. You could listen to musicians playing reggae, rock-and-roll, classical, or Afro-pop. You could sign petitions, register to vote, question political candidates, or volunteer to work for a worthy cause. And you could watch all manner of people, from grizzled quarriers in bib overalls to executives in suits to college students in cut-off jeans to Tibetan Buddhist monks in burgundy robes, all milling together and smiling, as they fill their bags and arms with bounty. They talk, touch, greet friends, dandle babies, exchange notes and promises; they shelter from the rain under pavilions or tilt their faces to the sun. In those faces you can read the pleasure that draws humans together into villages and cities, the delight in sharing words, food, beauty, and laughter.

This delight in the company of other people, so evident in farmers' markets, is another quality of captivating places. Unlike the private, often exclusive conviviality of clubs, the conviviality I'm talking about is *public*, open to people of all ages and classes and descriptions. A vital community provides many gathering spots, from auditoriums and barbershops and cafes to playgrounds and plazas and parks, where people are free to mix with neighbors and strangers; the more diverse the mixture, the more illuminating the experience is likely to be. As far back as we can trace human settlement, our ancestors created public spaces for the exchange of goods and ideas, such as the bazaars and courtyards of the ancient Near East or the agorae of ancient Greece. Here in America, town halls and village greens helped shape the ideals of democracy. Insofar as we have kept those ideals alive, we have done so through creating arenas where all citizens can enter and all voices can be heard.

A shopping mall is a poor imitation of these convivial places. True, anyone may enter a mall, but the space is owned by a corporation rather than by the community. It is not designed to bring people together but to separate them from their money. The stores, which may be found anywhere from Seattle to Shanghai, bear no relation to geography. None of the goods for sale was locally produced. None of the food served in the restaurants was locally grown. The recipes, like the window displays and piped-in music, have been imposed from some distant headquarters. There is no freedom of assembly, as you can find out by trying to protest the sale of sweatshop products or fur coats, and there is no freedom of expression, as you can find out by trying to circulate a petition against our nation's latest war. Unlike an open-air market, a shopping mall is cut off from the weather, the seasons, the cycles of daylight and dark; it might as well be a spaceship, for all the connection it has to the community or the planet.

In a genuine gathering space, people from all walks of life may argue and joke and swap stories and admire one another's babies and sympathize with one another's aches, all the while feeling at home. Indeed, such gathering spots extend our sense of home beyond the four walls where we happen to sleep. The true wealth of a community shows up not in the grandeur of private residences or shopping emporiums but in the quality of libraries, schools, museums, parks, courthouses, galleries, and other public arenas.

It should go without saying that we encounter real places not by gazing through windshields or by gaping at screens but by walking. Alluring places invite us to immerse ourselves, to open all our senses. Sidewalks become more important than streets; parks become more important than parking lots. On foot, we experience the world in three dimensions; we move at a speed that allows us to absorb and savor and reflect. By comparison, the world presented by the electronic media is disembodied, stripped down, anemic. To compensate for that impoverishment, the virtual world must become ever more hectic and sensational if it is to hold our attention. The actual world, the three-dimensional array of sights and textures and tastes and sounds that we find in a vibrant city or town, needs no hype in order to intrigue us.

What all of us long for, I suspect, is to love the places in which we live and to live in places worthy of love. Surrounded by sham and disarray, we hunger for integrity and authenticity. We wish to dwell *some*where rather than *no*where. The list of qualities that distinguish a real place from a phony one might be greatly extended. But I hope I have said enough to suggest why cities and towns endowed with a rich, deep, coherent sense of place might inspire visitors to nurture similar qualities back home. By carrying home the benefits of a journey, we complete the circle, we pass on the gift.

Tourism can avoid being merely another form of private consumption only if it preserves and celebrates the commonwealth of the place visited as well as the place to which the visitor returns. "Commonwealth" is a venerable word that has fallen out of use in our hyperindividualistic culture. On television, in advertising, from board rooms and podiums, we hear incessantly about private wealth, but we rarely hear about the wealth we share. Yet the well-being of individuals and of communities utterly depends on that shared wealth—clean air and water, fertile soil, good schools and libraries, safe streets, honest government, a fair system of laws, an abundance of public lands, access to the world's accumulation of knowledge and art, and countless other blessings that we inherit by virtue of our membership in the human family. Insofar as tourism enhances the commonwealth, it is a blessing; insofar as it depletes the commonwealth, it is a curse.

The sort of tourism we ought to encourage would show us the lives people lead together in a place, how they cooperate, make decisions, solve problems, enjoy one another's company, and look after their home ground. It would renew our appreciation for the security that arises from neighborliness and mutual aid. It would encourage us to think about our cities, towns, and countryside as arenas for our common life, and not merely as patchworks of private property. It would remind us that we are responsible for the care of our communities, for the health of the land, and for one another. In short, such tourism would educate us to become better citizens, first of our neighborhoods and ultimately of our nation and planet.

If my hopes seem high, perhaps you will understand why, when I tell you that I recently became a grandfather. The birth of that child set me thinking even harder about our responsibility to future generations. We have been given much, especially those of us with the freedom to travel, and we should feel duty bound to preserve the sources of those gifts. We should do everything we can to reinvigorate our waning democracy and to heal our damaged land. I realize that a revival of citizenship, with a renewed concern for the commonwealth, will require more than the most virtuous forms of tourism. But I also believe that civic tourism, rightly pursued, might help us turn toward a saner, kinder, more peaceful and equitable world. That is the world I want for my grandchildren, and for all children forever.

Scott Russell Sanders is Distinguished Professor of English at Indiana University. The author of more than twenty books, including the recent *A Private History of Awe*, he has received a Lannan Literary Award and many other prestigious honors. Dr. Sanders lives in Bloomington, Indiana, with his wife Ruth.

# MOUNTAIN PRELUDE
## *After Seeing the Green Fire Die*

*But oft, in lonely rooms, and 'mid the din*
*Of towns and cities, I have owed to them*
*In hours of weariness, sensations sweet,*
*Felt in the blood, and felt along the heart . . .*

~William Wordsworth, "Tintern Abbey"

*The Rite of Spring* pulses through the car as the sun inches over a ridge of two-lane blacktop ahead. Morning's slanted glare ricochets off tiny pale bursts, the winged guts of bugs splattered across the windshield, but even through these lifeless interferences the scene is embracing. I am safe, folded into hills.

Driving east of Helena, in the rolling transition between Montana's jagged mountain west and mostly horizontal east, I lower the window and reach into November's cold, jacket sleeve snapping as hand and arm glide on the hard air. Oily, damp Douglas fir and an indistinguishable clutter of musky animal scents fill the car. I turn down the music and Stravinsky's timpani-strings synchronization continues between the tire treads and a rowdy, slapping creek to my right. The water is rough, just wide enough that I'd have a tough time jumping over it and staying dry, and about a half degree and one week away from limping to a frozen stop.

I'm driving home to Arizona, stopping in southern Montana to discuss economic development with a town that most of its residents think of as either a "tourist attraction" or a "tourist trap," depending on their general attitude toward tourism. Like more than a few, this place could probably provide a better quality of life for locals and, just as well, build a healthier hospitality industry— economically, politically, socially—if it pulled back the camera and viewed tourism through a wider lens. That's a conversation I've had lately with a lot of communities, although I'm still hoping to stumble upon the camera angle from which to successfully capture the full scene.

For many places in this part of the country, tourism is one of the most important engines of the economy—if not *the* engine. The industry is a tremendous economic driver in every state in the nation, and in the West its significance is often more pronounced, due in part to the area's majestic natural and cultural landscapes. Joseph Wood Krutch called the West's *hereness* the "grandeur of something powerfully alien," where compelling, unique stories of land and people intertwine in evocative ways, providing a solid base for the hospitality sector to build on. That's not news, so it's no surprise most communities have hosted their share of tourism experts, while public officials and business leaders regularly attend travel and economic development confabs, from which they bring home laundry lists of tourism's "best practices." Good work is being done, yes, but some of the policy, sadly, seems scripted by consultants out of the pages of John Perkins's *Confessions of an Economic Hit Man*, who leave in their wake economic disparity, environmental ruin, and social ennui—at best. Just look around and then tell me that most places, especially rural towns embalmed in asphalt dowdiness and minimum-wage economies, are headed in the right direction. Regrettably, James Howard Kunstler's "geography of nowhere" has established itself—or, it's fairer to say, *we* have established *it*—as the norm, which is not welcome news for quality of life in general nor specifically for tourism, an industry that, historically, has benefited most from quality differentiation, not kitschy homogeneity.

Barely braking, but letting the car slow on the uphill, I steer onto the gravel shoulder, turn off the ignition, and breathe in deep. The rock-filled creek tumbles loud and the morning chatter of sparrows accompanies my long exhale. As I step from the car the wind starts to make itself difficult, and a distant out-of-place murmur grows. Then lights from over the ridge cut into the graying sky and a semi hurls past, lending a hand to the wind and forcing me to hold onto the open car door—momentarily a modern-day John Muir, swaying at the top of a Yosemite fir in a lightning storm, fist thrust to the sky above the roar, daring God to just *bring it on!* I am no Muir. Buffeted by cold and spectacle, I choose comfort and return to the car.

Directly ahead beyond the other side of the highway a cragged hillside looms, its mysterious interior, silhouetted tree tips, and granite contours beginning to betray murky snatches of deep green and slate. Standing at the bend, where the slope pushes the road right, a coyote catches my eye and I hers. No doubt she's crossing to the stream, a morning rite, but my presence creates pause, if only seconds. Ahead, lights and the same deep rumble, another truck races toward us, a nearly noiseless flash flashes before me, and the coyote lies twisted, shades of gray matted with black purple, her face bent downhill towards me.

> We reached the old wolf in time to watch a fierce green fire dying in her eyes. I realized then, and have known ever since, that there was something new to me in those eyes—something known only to her and to the mountain. I was young then and full of trigger-itch; I thought that because fewer wolves meant more deer, that no wolves would mean hunters' paradise. But after seeing the green fire die, I sensed that neither the wolf nor the mountain agreed with such a view.

So recalled forester Aldo Leopold in a 1944 essay, "Thinking Like a Mountain." A disciple of Gifford Pinchot's utilitarian land-management policies, Leopold had shot the mother wolf on a ridge in eastern Arizona in 1909, a routine act since the Forest Service's eradication policy of the day held that fewer predators benefited ranchers and left more deer for hunters. But the "fierce green fire" ebbing in the wolf's eyes planted a thought young Aldo did not fully grasp, let alone express, for decades: that a natural reciprocity already regulated the hillside absent his management theory. In that Arizona mountain moment the Yale-educated tenderfoot intuited at least some of this relationship and eventually became an eloquent voice for stewardship, speaking for all the "cogs and wheels" and advocating a communal approach to nature that we still haven't figured out how to implement. One stumbling block is that Leopold's appeal to think like a mountain, not a land manager, strikes readers as compelling, but it's slippery like a goldfish in a child's hands, escaping practical application. More than a few planning institutes and think tanks would like to decipher mountain thinking—"biomimicry" and "industrial ecology" are among the experimental approaches—and then translate the code for public policy. Me too. Mountains have figured it out. Nature works.

I don't know if the dead coyote is part of the mountain's deliberations or not since I, an outsider, am now implicated in the chain of events that led to the unhappy scene before me. Am I part of the thought that writes this land's story? Thinking too hard like a mountain in a setting like this could give me a headache, especially if I dwell on the fact that dramas like Leopold's wolf-deer-forest scenario are acted out on the damp hillside in front of me in more ways than any of us knows. Okay, dwell, a little:

Every fist-size clump of dirt is at this moment playing host to thousands of throbbing microbes—tiny transactions dancing, developing, decomposing. An inch of topsoil might represent several hundred years of labor by worms, ants, and other partners of the soil. Trees are their own universe, a big one sucking skyward tons of water and recreating "absolutely from scratch," marvels Annie Dillard, "ninety-nine percent of its living parts" *every year*. There could be more than two million species wedged into the spongy world before me, many still unknown and unnamed by us, all humming along, playing their part in the pulsing web of plants, insects, fungi, animals, and countless microorganisms that make up the mountainside, its face just beginning to collect the sunrise, a greeting that's occurred billions of times. Yeah, think like *that* mountain, think like the intelligence that thinks *that* design. Imagine how all the parts fit together, in almost infinite combinations, and be an impartial advocate for every one, even poison ivy, mosquitoes, parasites, and predators.

Leaving my refuge, I lean into the easterly, hands shoved deep in my pockets, and trudge through gray light to the other side of the road, where the "hobo of the hills," Mary Austin's nickname for the scrawny scavenger, lies bent, partly on and off the pavement. What would the mountain do? Kneeling, I mash a handful of brittle roadside leaves, open my fist, and let the wind scatter the crumbs over the coyote, a few sticking to her drying eyes. I look hard into their thickening fog for something like forgiveness, or a clue to an ancient place in the mountain's DNA—some reason for the randomness and apparent meaninglessness of this act. Maybe, as nineteenth-century botanist Lester Ward believed, nature *doesn't* make sense: moths fly into flames, bees die when they sting, opossums have more babies than teats, insects eat their young—and a coyote dies because I stopped. Waste, chaos, entropy, folly. What kind of model is that?

Not wishing to surrender to that gloom, I imagine I should do or say something noble here on the shoulder of this two-lane blacktop in central Montana—smear some ceremonial leaf dust inside her ear or hymn a blessing (*Nyaga mutzi*). But all I do is nudge the coyote off the road with my foot, walk back to the edge of the creek, stamp down a crackly tuft of frozen cattails, and rinse the bloodstain on my boot, a dance with tawny wandering leaves, while sparrows prattle above a loud lyric of channeled wind and water. A muffled snap interrupts my leaf gazing, and I glance upstream to catch a brown blur of animal, surely a spectator of this morning's episode, slithering into the dank brush while the creek presses on.

As it will tomorrow and the next day.

How long I'm fixed upstream, contemplating the end of a design that never comes, I don't know. "Eventually, the watcher joined the river," Norman Maclean mused about this very country, "and there was only one of us. I believe it was the river."

Belonging here is enough, and I should just let mountain thinking be. Coming to terms with his own mountain, Thoreau said as much: "The highest that we can attain to is not Knowledge, but Sympathy with Intelligence," which he reduced to "Contact! Contact!" Don't analyze, accept—the difference between knowing how a bicycle works and experiencing its balance for the first time, which comes finally when you give up thinking about it, give up trying to control it. And then it never betrays you.

So, butterflies taste with their feet. Go figure.

Back in the car I turn up the music and ease onto the rising road, the ridge ahead still shielding most of the sun, its first rays gathering on the mountain's highest outcroppings. As the smells, sounds, and shelter of the hills fade and Stravinsky's splendid coda becomes the soundtrack for my drive, a dead coyote and human impulse mingle in my thoughts, and I consider the town three hours down the road. How can the private awe behind me be decoded for other shared settings—built, cultural, natural? That'd be a pretty cool tourist attraction, one I'd pay to see.

Leopold said think like a mountain. Perhaps we can think like Aldo Leopold thinking about our communities, beginning with the phrase that honed his ethic: "love, respect, and admiration." Imagine. The PowerPoint presentation on my laptop won't do, and I start composing a different talk to myself as I drive out of the hills, over the crest and into the shimmering valley below. There, etched with care into the "great turrets of stone," local writer Ivan Doig's description of the Castle Mountains, the southbound road from White Sulphur Springs invites me home.

> We shall not cease from explorations
> And the end of all our exploring
> Will be to arrive where we started
> And know the place for the first time.

~T. S. Eliot, "Little Gidding"

# COMMUNITY
# CONVERSATIONS

# 1. FRAME FLIPPING:
## *Something More Than a Business*

*The community accomplishes the productive work that is necessary to any economy; the economy supports and preserves the land and the people. The economy cannot prey on the community because it is not alienated from the community; it is the community.*
~Wendell Berry, "Does Community Have Value?"

The subtitle of this essay—"the poetry and politics of place"—represents a twofold consideration (product and process) of an industry that, arguably, generates the most economic activity in your region; possesses tremendous potential to fiddle with the look and feel of your town; changes the social, economic, political, cultural, and environmental landscapes of nearly every place it touches; and increasingly is using the deep-rooted memories of your community's narrative (neighborhoods, cultures, natural wonders) as products—commodifying them and, in the process, sometimes altering meaning, occasionally rewriting history, certainly modifying form and content. Yet it is an industry that operates stealthily, with little public oversight, recognition, respect, or support.

That is changing. The business of tourism, which is among the top three economic drivers in every state in the nation, is too important and influential, in good ways and ill, to be left to the traditional "hospitality industry"—those who pave the way for, service, and take advantage of the visitor experience, whether for leisure, business, education, or escape. Given that hospitality-dependent economies continue to multiply, that local tourism decisions often affect residents more than visitors, and, further, that the tourism product increasingly is crafted from a region's "sense of place"—that is, the very thing people call *home*—it is essential that we deepen and broaden the conversation about if, how, and for what purpose communities "do" tourism. The following pages touch on why we should and how we can, incorporating three overlapping strategies that emerged during discussions with citizens in dozens of communities:

- rethink economics
- connect to the public
- invest in the story

The civic mission is not new. Indeed, since the 1970s a number of tourism scholars have recommended, Peter Murphy notes, "a more open and community-oriented approach which views tourism as a local resource." Our local conversations updated, amplified, and sharpened that charge by pulling together contemporary economic, social, and environmental place-making tenets, and then using tourism to unlock their potential and enhance their integration. If citizens appreciate *that* possibility for the industry, if they begin with a renewed sense of hopeful purpose, many of the mechanics will fall into place. There's no shortage of consultants, publications, organizations, foundations, and best practices to help communities rethink economics, connect to the public, and invest in the story. The *how* isn't scarce or unknown, perhaps there's another *why*. One close to home.

Undeniably, civic tourism is among a lengthy list of proposals that question more than a few accepted industry goals, structures, and procedures, so it comes as no surprise that some voices may not endorse the direction this conversation will take us. Ultimately, however, it is in your community's interest—*and*, others are discovering, in the local tourism community's interest—to look beyond the industry's dated, self-imposed, mission-driven boundaries and limitations. Often cutting deep and forging new fields of study, the academy has studied the "boundaries and limitations" of place-based tourism for several decades, and the research can read like someone describing a painting or symphony, maybe jazz. The painting is by Seurat, pointillism executed in dabs of culture, finance, nature, design, politics, and society. The symphony is by Stravinsky, pieces that can jar individually but work when folded together. Jazz speaks for itself, like a mountain I know. Skimming a bit of this research and folding it into our community discussions, this essay hopes to encourage the guardians and appreciators of place, *including* members of the traditional tourism cluster, to begin conversations that "look beyond" the industry's boundaries and limitations, not really knowing what you will find "beyond," but trusting that mountain thinking will lead communities to value and then act on a restorative tourism ethic, one that believes, as Aldo Leopold writes in "The Land Ethic," that a policy "based solely on economic self-interest is hopelessly lopsided. It tends to ignore, and thus eventually to eliminate many elements in the land community that lack commercial value, but that are (as far as we know) essential to its healthy functioning. It assumes, falsely, I think, that the economic parts of the biotic clock will function without the uneconomic parts."

### *A Dab of History*

It's worth remembering that as an "industry" (and there's plenty of debate about whether it even is such a thing) tourism is relatively young—still maturing, finding its way, learning how to belong as a responsible corporate citizen. Certainly people have always traveled to experience different places and cultures: thirteenth-century BCE Roman graffiti on Egyptian tombs, American Indian oral histories, Chaucer's fourteenth-century pilgrimage verse, accounts from Neoclassical aristocrats on the Grand Tour, and the nineteenth-century fascination with travel literature, such as Isabella Bird's immensely popular *A Lady's Life in the Rocky Mountains*, tell us that much. In my neck of woods, Fred Harvey revolutionized and popularized tours to Indian lands and national parks in the early twentieth century, Lorenzo Hubbell dabbled in trading post curios, and Route 66 towns such as Gallup, New Mexico, were defined by travel. They still are. Travel has often been part of our economy and work (the root is *travail*), and business has regularly lent a hand: guidebooks, transportation, lodging, souvenirs. But the everyday, ordinary experience of tourism has only come about in the average boomer's lifetime, which is also true of the way most municipalities practice tourism today—for example, funding convention and visitors bureaus and other taxpayer-subsidized enterprises to lure vacationing families and business travelers, in effect positioning the hospitality sector as integral to a region's overall development agenda. Considering the post–World War II era of development, it's not surprising that many of these operations were instinctively designed under the spell of industrial-age economics. Unfortunately, some planning, often where tourism is viewed as a panacea, is still intoxicated by that siren song, a tune that can shape cities and towns. Intersections dotted with cookie-cutter motels, chain restaurants, and gas stations blanket the landscape, joining with other uninspired development to change the very nature of public space. The assembly-line protocol, corporate supervision, and loyalty to one bottom line that characterizes these tourist stopovers regrettably may contaminate or otherwise sway general planning principles, reflected in Kunstler's pod worlds or Kenneth Jackson's "crabgrass frontier." When did this happen, and is tourism a cause or effect?

Set aside Europe and its centuries-long affair with mass tourism. Think about the place you were raised. Unless you lived in Atlantic City, Anaheim, Santa Fe, Scottsdale, Miami, a gateway community, a border town, a big city, or a handful of other places historically linked to travel, the industry was not a big deal in your community, especially rural places where "hospitality," such as it was, consisted of a gift shop, an outdoor supply store for weekend campers, and a batch of locally operated twelve-room motels on the edge of town. At restaurants my family frequented we saw neighbors, not strangers with cameras, and spotting cars with out-of-state licenses was a game my sister and I played. Our hometown's main drag consisted of a bunch of old houses; today a sign on the interstate, which didn't exist back then, welcomes travelers to "Historic Downtown." Sure, there were tourists—the decrepit billboard promoting our caves drew a few—but hardly anyone gave much thought to developing the industry into a keystone of the economy. Ours was a factory town. Seldom did an ambitious, publicly financed meta-machine annually dream up another scheme to attract traveling families to the area; rarely did governments, business associations, or universities conduct research to evaluate and exploit the staying habits of tourists; and almost never did public officials, corporate leaders, cultural advocates, and other community voices assemble in focus groups to brainstorm cutting-edge tourism strategies. I never saw a television commercial inviting my family to visit another state (developed and paid for by a public agency), newspapers had yet to publish travel sections that rival the classifieds' heft, and the Travel Channel and Expedia were decades away. As recently as a generation or two ago, a great deal of local travel business was managed, if that's even the right word, by default. Appeals to expend public funds to advertise hotels and other private attractions were greeted as "corporate welfare" (still true in places), while city planners dismissed tourism as a harmless but economically irrelevant boutique industry—the equivalent of your little nephew, seated at the children's table for Thanksgiving dinner. There now, Sonny, we've got *important* things to discuss.

But somewhere along the line tourism snuck up on us when we were reaching for the gravy and joined the adults at the big table, becoming one of the largest industries in the world, and a lot of slick salesmen convinced local officials that *your* town deserved a piece of the pie—and, hey, it's a clean industry! Nice people visit, spend money, and go home; and we can tax *them* to pay for *our* services! Dandy. With dollar signs clouding our vision, we allowed industrial-age tourism, gradually, like the frog in boiling water, to infiltrate, influence, and in some cases take control of social and economic policymaking; and now some of us look around and notice that much of what we don't like about our dowdy drive-thru landscape can be traced to an industry that serves strangers and corporate bottom lines. Not us. Many who care about "place," the very thing the traveling public is supposedly interested in experiencing, have seen their hospitality industry snookered or even hijacked by forces that are not entirely friendly to place-making: "The fault, dear Brutus, is not in our stars, / But in ourselves, that we are underlings." In *Devil's Bargains*, his history of western tourism communities, Hal Rothman describes a familiar endgame:

> In each, the new configuration changed the balance of power, granting incoming neonatives a greater say in the direction of the town than its longtime residents possessed. The process alienated locals, many of whom did not understand and few of whom could participate in the changes. The neonatives who were attracted to these transformed places soon recast them as reflections of their values.

## A Restorative Tourism

In these conversations, then, I'd like to talk about why I believe it is incumbent upon and possible for your local tourism sector, revivified and retooled, to emerge as a leading force for economic, social, environmental, cultural, and political change. Small stuff like that. These aren't comfy conversations—asking tourism and cultural professionals to reexamine and possibly reshuffle long-held priorities, to rebuild and reinforce the decision-making and financial scaffolding, to entertain concepts that may seem irrelevant to the business of tourism, and to operate responsibly, transparently, and deferentially with the public. For some in the travel business it's likely more fun to think about designing a new visitors guide or tinker with a website and, as a result, this conversation goes nowhere. Elsewhere museum directors say they're too busy and, anyway, they've already done the cultural tourism thing. Or civic tourism is too conceptual, theoretical, and academic; it's not practical, raises more questions than it answers, and doesn't provide enough best practices. Others say I'm naive and don't understand how business really works—Spencer had it right.

That is all true. Designing a marketing campaign probably is more enjoyable than wandering through an unknown and sometimes threatening territory; opening operations to the public can be fraught with angst, especially in towns where tourism is not well liked; I do lay out a lot of problems and don't deliver as many answers; there's no guarantee these conversations will accomplish anything, partly because they deal in slippery topics like people's values; it's surely less risky to adopt best practices that work elsewhere, projects thought through and delivered FedEx; and, yes, I'm just naive enough to think that tourism can be bigger than the tawdry and inequitable business practices that threaten the very things people love about their communities—that tourism can be, in fact, a transformative agent.

What makes me think so is that it's happening. We are beginning to see exciting, sustainable, community-directed, economically robust place-based tourism initiatives around the world, centered in the interactions between and among the hospitality sector, nonprofit organizations, government, and, most importantly, a proud, committed public. These efforts are proof that building vibrant communities *touristically*, to warp Dean MacCannell's invented term even more, is indeed a hope that is not misplaced. A few of these models are mentioned here, and we need more of them, but civic tourism, which itself is an experiment that will no doubt look different by the time these words see print, is not so much a menu of best practices as it is sketchy directions to the kitchen, where you're invited to discover and concoct your own recipes. Place, Melville reminds us, "is not on any map," so especially when place is the product, tourism and the communities in which the industry does its business are often shortchanged by the prescriptive, copycat approach, jumping to schemes that appear to work elsewhere before examining one's own circumstances, one's own values. That's old advice:

> . . . before we plow an unfamiliar patch
> It is well to be informed about the winds,
> About the variations in the sky,
> The native traits and habits of the place.
> What each locale permits, and what denies.
> ~Virgil, *The Georgics*

Determining what constitutes and befits your "native traits and habits of the place," and *who gets to say*, is the process civic tourism embraces—the "poetry and politics of place." Destination communities have long weighed similar questions, but nearly always from a perspective that interprets the possibility of tourism narrowly—as an economic apparatus, as a tool that serves visitors. The pervasiveness of tourism today, however, combined with its increasing reliance on place-based attractions, especially among smaller communities where tourism historically has been a marginal player, argues for a broader interpretation of the industry's instrumentality.

### Triple Bottom Line

Our local conversations exhibited a double-edged theme: In communities where "sense of place" has tourism appeal the hospitality industry is often perceived as either a corporate juggernaut that threatens to undermine a region's identity, or an ineffective economic catalyst, unable to capitalize on the area's intrinsic assets. Or both, often combined with a wish to do it right. Given the growth of hospitality-dependent economies among small to mid-sized towns, these places, which represent the majority of communities, are often the most vulnerable, yet they also hold the greatest potential to craft a responsible tourism ethic, from which citizens can build a sustainable travel economy. It's hard to wrap my mind around Las Vegas or towns that want to be Vegas, or the theme-park complexes, cruise-ship ports, and resort capitals of the globe, although there are neighborhoods and initiatives *within* these larger vacation megalopolises that may benefit from these conversations, such as Las Vegas's efforts to diversify its travel options by highlighting the city's wonderful cultural facilities and overlooked dramatic desert setting—a happy development to be sure. No one sitting in my chair denies the significance of mass travel; there's a place for Mickey Mouse, wax museums, Dollywood, and the rest of that synthetic bait. That "place," however, should be a concentrated exception that feeds local tourism economies rather than a model to which others aspire. Big calculated tourism is just not feasible, nor is it usually suitable at any scale, for many smaller communities where hospitality programs struggle, often because they're hoodwinked into measuring success against Gatlinburg's traffic or Orlando's balance sheet. Listen up: You already have a theme park! It's called your streetscape, your lands, your cultures, and *no other community possesses those same gifts*. Forget about being Santa Fe—be yourself first. Forget about attracting or appealing to visitors—satisfy your residents first.

The belief that tourism isn't living up to the boosters' hype, owing to one or both conditions cited above, runs through a lot of places, some of which I've visited, and after meeting in dozens of towns with hundreds of people, I believe this: Encouraged to mature *organically*, that is, humbly, in a manner appropriate to and consistent with a region's heritage, and *ecologically*, that is, reciprocally, in true partnership with other community players, the hospitality industry has the potential to transform towns—to create prosperous, sustainable, dynamic, distinctive *places*. Talking about tourism this way, as *the* agent for social, cultural, environmental, and economic regeneration, is a values discussion, not an inventory of best practices or toolbox of paint-by-number techniques, but that's the center from which a responsible tourism ethic must spring, starting with core principles—*what we value, what we aspire to*—not more "projects," a new brand, or better marketing. What I have in mind is a large shift, beginning close by.

Now is the appropriate time for tourism—*especially at the local level, where adjustments are usually easier and more effectual*—to redefine its purposes and methods using values-based strategies that do not answer solely to the economic bottom line, but to social and environmental bottom lines as well, a tripartite scheme that encompasses "The Three Es": ecology, economy, and equity. First defined by John Elkington as the "triple bottom line," this characteristic of contemporary economic theory revives and amplifies John Kenneth Galbraith's concern in his 1958 classic, *The Affluent Society*: the nonfinancial responsibilities of financial activities. Adopting a holistic, restorative approach to community planning where the market, to cite Paul Hawken, "creates, increases, nourishes and enhances" regional culture can enrich quality of life across the board, including economic health.

Happily for tourism, *no industry is better suited to benefit from and make a worthy contribution to triple-bottom-line research and development.* But to do so, local hospitality leaders and practitioners must step forward and own it, which means rewiring what success looks like, embracing another set of values, and partnering with a different cast of characters—redefining, in fact, what constitutes your "tourism industry." Just the same, these new partners, soldiers in the place brigade—cultural organizations, preservation agencies, and land-use groups, to name a few—should walk through the door that has been nudged open for them by today's creative economists and join the conversation—and *not* in a token capacity, since they, not the travel bureau, are what visitors come to experience. Also, as Aldo Leopold discovered while hoping to advance an ethic that reframed humankind's relationship to the larger biotic community, another essential ingredient in the conversation, perhaps the most essential, is the civic sphere: "We need knowledge— public awareness—of the small cogs and wheels," he realized.

Civic tourism extends Leopold's ecological and political expressions to the process of place-making for touristic purposes. Just as his many writings, and especially the classic *A Sand County Almanac*, magnify biological and historical relationships *in* and ethical responsibilities *to* nature, so too, argues sociologist Robert Bellah and his coauthors in *Habits of the Heart*, is there something like a "social ecology," a network of cultural reciprocities that distinguishes our communities, a network from which the travel sector has too often stood apart. Thinking like Leopold's mountain, wedging tourism into a comprehensive causal framework, reveals this about the industry's prospects in your community: Its most opportunistic links to quality economic growth strategies, such as those advanced by triple-bottom-line lingo, are vertical and multi-layered, cyclical rather than linear, and comparative rather than reductionist, not unlike ecosystems in nature. "Economics requires the *comparison* of costs and benefits," emphasizes Herman Daly, "*not their addition*." Considering tourism development as part of a complex, interrelated whole, where economic reciprocity is evaluated within a values-based bubble, is the first step toward reimagining the industry's potential, the key to reframing tourism's purpose. Mountain thinking moves tourism into a network where relationships, and relationships between relationships, matter, especially between and among economic, environmental, and social structures—the three-legged stool of triple-bottom-line planning and, not insignificantly, the three primary legs of tourism development. A healthy place and a sustainable tourism economy rest, together, atop a level stool. Today, most are tilting.

## A Way Cool Something Else

Many of tourism's restraints, as well as its unflattering reputation, spring from the industry's tacit connection to and sanctioning of the growth machine, a term coined by economist Harvey Molotch in his 1976 essay, "The City as a Growth Machine: Toward a Political Economy of Place." It's no coincidence that many hospitality operations, whether local or statewide, are housed within and managed by a chamber of commerce, department of commerce, or similar marketing or economic development agency, whose letterhead slogan or public relations meme typically includes words like *jobs* or *more* or *growth*—perhaps all three in some combination—and whose respective boards of directors and advisory councils are liberally sprinkled with members who benefit from the triumph of that slogan, people Molotch refers to as "politically mobilized local elites": developers, realtors, hoteliers, bankers, media owners, retailers, car dealers, politicians, and other usual suspects.

The implication is beyond implied: tourism is about dollars. And that's okay, to a point. Justifiably, the economic argument will always remain a weapon in the hospitality sector's advocacy arsenal—when lobbying for public funds, for example. Once, though, when I was doing just that a friendly legislator whose ear I was bending leaned close and said, "Dan, everybody here makes the economic argument—health care, universities, transportation, corrections, social services, you name it. What else you got?" Well, tourism's got something else, a *way cool* something else, but somewhere along the way we misplaced it. Yes, Thomas Cook started his tours in the 1840s to make money, which they did and still do, but he also imagined his trips would benefit the struggling working class and bring people of different backgrounds together, thereby averting misunderstandings between nations.

In that same spirit today proponents of cultural tourism, heritage tourism, geotourism, sustainable tourism, community tourism, ecotourism, and a long, growing, and sometimes perplexing list of other alternative approaches to travel, including unabashedly political ventures such as social justice tourism and peace tourism, imagine the hospitality business as *something more* than a business, as something other than the market-driven "reign of quantity" that E. F. Schumacher warned can destroy what we love: "The modern industrial system, with all its intellectual sophistication, consumes the very basis on which it has been erected. To use the language of the economist, it lives on irreplaceable capital which it cheerfully treats as income." Does the whaling industry ring a bell? Or consider the question Jared Diamond asks in *Collapse*: "What did the Easter Islander who cut down the last palm tree say while he was doing it? Like modern loggers, did he shout 'Jobs, not trees!'?"

Radical when introduced more than thirty years ago, and still pooh-poohed by textbooks, trickle-downers, and global free-marketers clinging to Adam Smith's invisible hand, Schumacher's Buddhist Economics nonetheless resonates with today's triple-bottom-line proposals, some of which are bracketed within labels like "New Economy," "Creative Economy," or "Green Economy." For the hospitality industry, the implications of this trend are indeed cautionary, given the sector's industrial bent, seemingly designed by Ayn Rand, yet also extremely promising, since the New Economy and a responsible tourism ethic dance around the same pinpoint—*place*. Communities have a choice, reminiscent of the one confronting the Western world in the nineteenth century as the Industrial Revolution roared across the land: Either use technology's inventions to spur hope and collective progress, the position of Beatrice Webb's Fabian Society, or succumb to the cynicism of Herbert Spencer's cutthroat social Darwinism and its corollary laissez-faire marketplace, whose comeuppance Garrett Hardin forecasts in his famous essay, "Tragedy of the Commons," where dog-eat-dog policies eventually devour *all* the dogs—or cattle, in Hardin's story. The hospitality industry can learn from past misreadings and misapplications of Darwin, who wrote *not* of "survival of the fittest" in Spencer's gloomy individualistic idiom, but of variation, adaptation, and cooperation in place-based contextual terms. Go, Chuck.

Respecting the caution while capitalizing on the hope and promise, civic tourism stakes out a bit of new territory, since the relevant economic models of our day, the offspring of Webb, Galbraith, Schumacher, Jane Jacobs, and other early progressive scholars and activists, rarely mention the hospitality sector, one of the most powerful economic machines in the world, focusing instead on nurturing high tech utopias and similar "knowledge economies," or on retrofitting industries historically unfriendly to place—energy, transportation, and manufacturing, for example. Too, some New Economy–speak comes down from the macro peripheries of academic theory, not up from the street-level transactions that distinguish local tourism operations. Other studies privilege the politics of globalization over grassroots activism that might reshape perceptions and, perchance, universal policies. Elsewhere the language leans toward manufacturing hip Pottery Barn villages for the gentrified set, not real places for real people. Most interestingly, the New Economy has little room for tourism, which in today's fashionable literature occupies a low rung on the ladder of economic respectability. At the same time, it must be said, the hospitality industry has made but few creative attempts to move up the ladder: "The main mistake made by pro-tourist planners," writes Dean MacCannell, "is they see tourism only in traditional economic terms"—that is, one bottom line.

Civic tourism addresses these omissions and discrepancies with a creed that accepts, even celebrates, the omnipresence and continuing growth of travel, the power of place, and the possibility of citizen politics. An extension of, supplement to, and tool for heritage tourism, ecotourism, and other place-enhancing designs, civic tourism suggests another way into the local hospitality conversation—a way of conducting tourism planning as *community* planning; a way of locating the hospitality industry as a *solution* to healthy place-making, rather than an obstacle; and a way of valuing and practicing tourism as a *public art*, with all of the social and ethical obligations embedded in that undertaking. That is, a tourism "reframed," reversing and turning inside out the conventional paradigm, as Wendell Berry advises: "The answers to the human problems of ecology are to be found in economy. And the answers to the problems of economy are to be found in culture and in character." That's a good place to start.

"Reframing is changing the way the public sees the world," writes linguist George Lakoff. Civic tourism urges your community, beginning with the caretakers of place, to help change the way the public sees tourism: as a *means* and not an end. "For all their power and vitality," the authors write in *Natural Capitalism*, "markets are only tools. They make a good servant but a bad master and a worse religion." It's one thing to talk about tourism as a "means" or "tool," but acting on that talk is a huge and difficult frame flip, and it's not a mission statement you'll find embossed on the letterhead of too many travel and tourism bureaus. Your state office of tourism, for example, is a research and marketing agency, and probably a good one, but it's definitely focused on economic ends and place-making is not its job. But it's yours if you want it, and especially at the local level tourism gives citizens a tool, when held in their hands, to build the kind of place where they want to live, work, and raise a family. Ultimately, a "civic" approach can embolden sense of place, the local economy, *and* tourism's social ties and political standing, a not unwelcome change for an industry that's usually talked about, if at all, as a necessary evil among residents or the Rodney Dangerfield of economic development among planners and politicians.

### Possibility Unbound: Juicy Peaches

Former World Bank economist Herman Daly writes, "The economy is a subsystem of the environment," a reminder that all commercial activities, not just agriculture, mineral extraction, and other obvious land-based businesses, are dependent on the natural and cultural landscapes in which they find themselves. Nowhere is that more true than with the tourism industry, where, like farming and other trades rooted in the land, we sow, nurture, harvest; and we neglect "the habits of the place," as Virgil coached farmers two thousand years ago, at our peril. Let us begin community conversations, as does peach farmer David Mas Masumoto, "by planting hope":

> In trying to save my Sun Crest peaches, I discover that they are more than just food, they are part of a permanence, a continuity with the past. People who enjoy my peaches understand what juicy, sweet ones taste like. Biting into one may send them back to the orchards of their childhoods and that warm sense of constancy of family found in their memories. Individuals leave for the city, but the memories of farms stay behind to anchor personal family histories.
>
> My peaches find a home with these folks, a touchstone to their past.

May you grow organic, juicy communities that "find a home" with visitors *and* residents.

# "Frame Flipping": Conversation Starters

1. **Background:** What has been the history of tourism development in your region? What agency or agencies oversee tourism? Why them? Is tourism a valuable part of the local economy? If so, when did that happen and what were the forces behind the industry's growth? Analyze the visitor guides and other materials distributed by the local tourism bureau. What do they say about your town? Your residents? What values do they promote? (Douglas Coupland writes in *Shampoo Planet*, "You might consider checking out the travel brochures for the town in which you live. You might be amazed. You might not want to live there anymore.")

2. **Stakeholders:** Peruse the names on the boards of directors and advisory commissions that oversee tourism development in your area. Are they primarily from the growth and development sector, or are there voices that represent environmental causes, historic preservation, education, and other social and cultural fields? How present is local government? Are tourism planning meetings open to residents? Does the lead agency offer avenues for public input: meetings, websites and blogs, surveys?

3. **Issues:** Are there controversial issues looming in your community that relate to tourism development? Does an outside firm, for example, want to build a timeshare complex on park land? Is traffic too congested or are property values soaring? Is there a sense that outsiders control policymaking? Whatever the issue, who resolves it? How does the public discuss it? At city council meetings, where roads, education, jobs, crime, and other topics are discussed, is tourism part of these deliberations? In other words, is town policy distinct from tourism policy, and vice versa?

4. **Book Discussion Idea:** *Epitaph for a Peach: Four Seasons on My Family Farm* by David Mas Masumoto (1995). Sponsor a community discussion with this award-winning book about raising peaches, and ask participants to apply Masumoto's philosophy to tourism development. That's one way to get inside this mountain thinking stuff.

# 2. RETHINK ECONOMICS:
## *Forsaking the Upstream Row*

*If the local people develop regional self-consciousness that transcends their immediate social situation and reflexive cultural structures, the tourists come in advance of the entrepreneurs, and a "cottage tourism industry" of the sort found in Ireland creates a more direct link between the money from tourism and local economic development. I am suggesting, then, that the industrial or plantation version of tourism is economically short-sighted. Eventually the capital that is generated by the natural growth tourism will succeed that of promoted, plantation tourism.*
~Dean MacCannell, *The Tourist: A New Theory of the Leisure Class*

One difficulty with putting all of tourism's marbles in the growth basket is that, ironically, doing so is economically counterproductive, because the industry is almost always a contributor to economic development efforts, giving more than it gets. It's not unusual to hear representatives of cultural attractions grumble about being exploited by the travel industry ("Disneyfication" and "commodification of culture" are popular refrains), but the industry itself is equally exploited by the larger development regime. The tourism experience often does not benefit from, and in fact is sometimes tripped up by, the supplicants of the growth machine, who can wreck places, undermine hospitality, and foster "uneconomic development"—dollars churn and transactions transact, but the practice dilutes the job base and profits skip town ("leakage"), while local budgets are redirected toward more highways, maintenance, infrastructure, and parking lots, stretched beyond their ability to serve residents, unable to preserve the reasons people moved there in the first place.

Influential voices nonetheless continue to chant the mantra that hospitality is nourished by the machine, that "more" is always "better" for those in the travel business, from restaurateurs to airline executives, consultants to advertisers, bankers to gift shop owners, and those who work alongside them. Even in towns where hospitality seems to have carved out an appropriate and manageable niche, where the industry is but one of several profitable economic clusters, the governing tourism ethic is still "do more." As a result, most meaningful tourism discussions take place within the growth frame, and the questions considered by industry leaders are usually debated and resolved within that same frame.

Civic tourism is about changing the frame. The first step in doing so doesn't require new projects, additional marketing, or more attractions, but a communal shift in perception: "Things don't change. You change your way of looking, that's all," wrote Carlos Castaneda. In the 1960s, sociologists defined this "way of looking" as a social construction: "the varying ways in which realities of the world are shaped," explain Schneider and Ingram. To illustrate how social

APPLICATION 3.2

constructions can serve as a catalyst for changing the way we perceive, value, and act—and that's precisely what we'd like to influence with respect to local tourism operations—sociologists have described the effect of the Earth views captured by Apollo 17 in 1972. The new perspective on our planet—showing it for the first time as a living, breathing, integrated orb—is credited with lending visual credence to *Silent Spring* and other ecological texts, and contributing to the public's deepening environmental consciousness. The famous "Blue Marble" photo triggered a collective "Aha!" moment.

Civic tourism encourages communities to pull back the camera, take a step or two sideways, and imagine a different social construction for the hospitality industry. That shift begins with rethinking economic policy for tourism, which turns on the question, "What do we want to sustain and for whom?" Gift shops for strangers or mountains for residents? That's an unfair "either/or" oversimplification, of course, because in a healthy tourism economy the two buttress one another. But encouraging "both/and" does not erase the priority question, if priorities have to be set, and they do, if only to counterbalance the machine's babbling about "jobs or the environment." The idolaters of growth have made their choice, and the "either/or" frame has served them well, wrong as it is.

The operating principle here is that sustaining growth-oriented components that *facilitate* the travel experience, often businesses that have no relevance to the place or its residents other than a commercial link, must be secondary and supplemental to sustaining and enhancing heritage-based products that *provide* the experience, assets which possess environmental, social, and economic value. This Three E or triple-bottom-line policy distinguishes "building buildings" from "building capacity"—one a short-term edict that simply, and recklessly, encourages more, the latter improving what's there so as to prepare for and adapt to change over the long haul. The virtuosos of "more" mainly want to sustain what they're doing, which by definition is unsustainable if we think of sustainability in the classic sense of living off the interest, not the principal. Consequently, hospitality operations bedded down with the growth industry are usually defined and governed by an A=B reductive logic that mandates attracting enough tourists (and workers) to sustain and ultimately expand the "facilitator economy." Even towns that purport to practice sustainable tourism often privilege, as one popular destination's mission statement confirms, "the long-term health of the industry." Put aside the jobs or bed-tax masquerades, both of which are tools to advance the primary ethic: expand the facilitator economy to attract and serve even more tourists because doing so nurtures the overall growth agenda. Gift shops for strangers.

The goals of facilitators and preservationists are not always mutually exclusive and occasionally they overlap, as in the case of a historic hotel or distinctive commercial or housing district that contribute to a region's identity—assets that locals value as well. But *that's* the conversation you should be having: Frame tourism planning for visitors as community planning for residents, that is, tourism policy as inseparable from town policy. Design a healthy place for the people who live there and tourists *will* come, on your terms; design your place to attract tourists and you might succeed in doing so, but unintended consequences may also ruin the qualities residents cherish. "Tourism planning as community planning" means travel-related activity is framed from the outset as a tool to sustain "great good places" agreed upon by the community, to borrow Ray Oldenburg's language, and only secondarily the facilitators—businesses that, ideally, follow in the wake of successful place-making, not the other way around. In other words, don't encourage motel construction or fast-food franchises to attract more tourists, provide jobs, or generate taxes, and then design your hospitality program to fill rooms and sell Big Macs—trying to engineer tourism, as Leopold sought to engineer nature before joining the mountain team. Quantity visitation rarely translates into quality experiences (insert your favorite tourist trap here); many new jobs will be taken by people who move to town *for* the job; and those taxes are already earmarked for extra security, roads, utilities, and other infrastructure mandated by the new construction.

Designing your tourism agenda around growing and sustaining the facilitator economy, rather than natural and cultural assets, is a backwards scheme that risks undermining your sense of place, relations with the public, *and* a healthy economy—the reverse of triple-bottom-line logic. Build the motels and restaurants when the success of your place-based travel program necessitates it, and then do so within the parameters of Virgil's "habits of the place," so as not to jeopardize the very thing visitors come to experience. Search for ways, whether aesthetic, social, or financial, that demonstrate how the facilitator economy can serve your preservation agenda, such as enacting a "green tax" or designating a portion of impact fees for parks or museums. The growth industry and its water carriers may fight and lobby against such proposals, but a revivified tourism community, guided by triple-bottom-line reasoning and reinforced with citizen voices, should come down on the side of the New Economy, a huge part of which is wedded to "place"—parks, not parking lots.

## *The Tourism Tango*

Centered firmly in *that* space, and working from *that* core value outward, the tourism community should aggregate and apply its considerable finances, connections, opportunities, and smarts to take towns, cities, and regions to heights of remarkable success, for the people who live in these places as well as short-term guests. Adding to the industry's chances for economic growth—and there's little doubt tourism is among the world's leading money makers (with a bullet)—is a growing list of contemporary development strategies, such as the triple-bottom-line doctrine, that are readymade for a tango with tourism.

32

Regrettably, mass-minded hospitality strategists are late to the dance and, just the same, the rock stars pushing these economic policies seldom mention the travel sector—or when they do it's in dismissive whispers, mostly because the industry has yet to prove them wrong. But it could.

I refer to trends like the New Economy and Creative Economy, large topics with many offshoots that appear in some guise or another on the agenda of nearly every urban planning meeting or economic development conference. Consult the work of John Howkins or Richard Florida, the movement's most sought-after guru, and you'll find statements such as, "The Creative Class lifestyle comes down to a passionate quest for experience," or, "The Creative Class is drawn to more organic and indigenous street-level culture." Similarly, Ray and Anderson's best-selling account of "Cultural Creatives" documents a large segment of the population who "demand that we go beyond environmental regulation to real ecological sustainability, to change our entire way of life accordingly." In his discussion of eco-efficiency DuPont CEO Charles Holliday, Jr. writes, "Customers are rejecting 'radical' materialism" in favor of values like community and authenticity; Robinson and Godbrey say in *Time for Life* that many of us are shifting from the "consumption of goods" to the "consumption of experiences"; while whole-brain dude Daniel Pink states, "the pursuit of purpose and meaning has become an integral part of our lives." Keep tourism in mind as you read Pink's prescription for business in the twenty-first century: "Mere survival today depends on being able to do something that overseas knowledge workers can't do cheaper, that powerful computers can't do faster, and that satisfies one of the nonmaterial, transcendent desires of an abundant age."

In effect, these and other economists and social observers validate and encourage what is at the core of place-based tourism: an authentic, meaningful, innovative, sustainable experience. So there *should* be a natural umbilical between the New Economy and hospitality. However, almost none of the progressive development literature nods in the slightest towards tourism, and in the few instances Florida alludes to it he cautions cities not to wander down that path where, he suggests, they'll find little more than a subsidized service industry encased in a low-wage bubble that privileges quantity not quality, façade not essence, visitors not residents—the very opposite of the New Economy manifesto. Who can blame him for thinking so? Look about. Perfectly positioned to adopt and exploit restorative economic policy, whose key theme is the authentic experience, local tourism programs remain mired in industrial-age muck, the one-dimensional, assembly-line thinking that wrecked America's smokestack cities, those like Detroit that neglected social and environmental consequences in blind pursuit of more widgets. Similarly, the question that tops the agenda at most local tourism planning meetings is not, "How can we improve our quality of life?" but something on the order of, "What can we do or build to attract more visitors?" Paul Hawken calls this an "immature" economic practice, where businesses "exchange stability and sustainability for short-term abundance and production." You're lucky if that doesn't sound familiar.

Richard Florida's glancing criticisms pale in comparison to the hordes of other tourism detractors, whose views industry leaders should not slough off so aloofly, because they are sometimes right. My intent, though, is not to pile more trash on the heap of blame or wallow too long in industry evils, as scores of studies already document these woes. Several, like *Devil's Bargains*, Rothman's Faustian indictment, have attained near seminal status among no-growthers and other industry naysayers intent on keeping the travel economy from further rooting itself in their towns. Publications such as the *Journal of Sustainable Tourism* regularly itemize the industry's nastier spillovers and byproducts, as do mainstream titles like the *Journal of Travel Research*. Tourism Concern and other watchdog organizations issue reports, manage websites, and host conferences that examine the sadder side of hospitality—from sex slaves and environmental degradation to the loss of local traditions and the general breakdown of society, including the economic inequities that make it difficult for hospitality employees to live in the very towns they serve. Most of that discussion, however, is centered in academic or activist circles, rarely making its way to official booster platforms at any level— national, state, and certainly not local. I've met city administrators and chamber of commerce directors who, with the wave of a hand, dismiss the findings in these troubling analyses, but I seldom meet many who have confronted the literature, and I've never encountered a session at a local hospitality conference that seriously engages the critiques. What are we afraid of? Tourism can and should answer with bold action, not just more of the same economic aspirin it's been dispensing.

While economists, tourism's stakeholders, and academics continue to debate the findings and methodologies, after several decades of research it seems clear that more travelers today, especially boomers, prefer life-enhancing experiences to sun, shopping, and entertainment distractions. Not all but enough. Now consider these vacationing habits in light of the shifting demographics and progressive, place-enhancing economic policies: The social, environmental, cultural, and economic stars are aligned, and, to mix even more metaphors, the fruit is hanging low. It is time for this adolescent industry to grow up, pull its head out of the fiscal quicksand that keeps sucking it under, and retune its priorities, especially on Main Street USA. The thing is, the critics are not far off the mark when they say "industrial tourism," as Edward Abbey disdainfully branded it nearly half a century ago, can ruin economies, built and natural environments, and social networks. Can it? Yes, and there's ample evidence. Does it have to? No, and that's the point. Your community has a choice, which Florida and others overlook or don't believe is possible. Some of us do.

That choice begins by "reframing" tourism's purpose, starting with the economic justifications underpinning that purpose. At a basic level ask, "*Why do we do tourism?*" Are the comings and goings of guests little more than a cheerleading backdrop for a rapacious growth policy that pays slight, if any, attention to its costs and consequences—chewing up, as Scott Sanders observes in his introduction, finite resources in pursuit of empty indulgences? Or can you imagine tourism as an *enabler* of healthy place-making, a *tool* for meaning-making, and a *means* to provide the sense of purpose and connection more people seek? It's not just retiring boomers who are searching for their own travel epiphanies, and it's not only Machu Picchu that can dish it out. Tourism isn't going away; it's not *if* you do it but *how*. Get in the game, but establish your own rules.

## Oars Up

Misreading tourism's potential is not the only drawback with some New Economy voices, whose cappuccino approach to urban planning may have but passing relevance for many suburban and rural burgs that are never going to land a Google branch office or university think tank—and in many regions that means most communities. Their original source of livelihood, often a factory or extractive industry such as mining, has petered out, and now some of these towns feel shackled to industrial-age tourism, caught in an economic spiral, dragged toward Leopold's "downhill equilibrium," a place whose policies and outcomes will not attract many high-value employers. Tourism is a "clean industry" elected officials were told decades ago, only to discover later that it can leave behind something nearly as toxic as iron ore tailings: container motels, trinket economies, a car-dependent culture, McDisneyization, social stratification, and billboarded horizons that obliterate the sense of place many residents only remember in their scrapbooks.

Try as they might, most of these places may never become Portland, Austin, San Francisco, Boston, Seattle, or other trendy bohemian paradises worshiped from the New Economy pulpit. But dig beneath the academic lingua franca and New Urbanist blueprints to the kernel of the modern message, and there is something within reach and worth pursuing for any community: that given a choice—and this process is entirely about choice-making—most people would prefer to live and work in distinctive, authentic, socially vibrant, economically diverse, educationally advanced, and environmentally wholesome *places*. Civic tourism simply (or maybe "not so simply") acknowledges that for some towns it is their hospitality industry, an industry tied to "sense of place" like no other, and not a high-tech idea economy, that is the nearest and most appropriate tool to help citizens conceptualize and then make that choice. But somebody has to say so, and then you have to act so.

The nut of New Economy dogma, the "kernel" I mention, is the same one Jane Jacobs, one of Florida's mentors, planted in the early 1960s, railing against the "monotonous, unnourishing gruel" of urban design, and then for decades persuasively linking her passion for diversity to economic policy. It's the kernel that animates the work of Kunstler, Lucy Lippard, and Ray Oldenburg, who underscore not only the "look and design" of a place, similar to Jacobs and her New Urbanist disciples, but what that look means for the economy, culture, and social relations—in the largest sense, what it means for democracy. And it's the kernel that distinguishes triple-bottom-line policy and other restorative strategies which acknowledge and exploit, in the best sense of that verb, the connections between environments and financial systems, most of which, because of their place-saving mission, are ripe for tourism's plucking: Herman Daly's ecological economics; Paul Hawken's ecology of commerce; the Lovins's natural capitalism; the asset-based theories of Nobel Prize-winning economist Amartya Sen; Daniel Pink's whole-brain calculus; the practices of civic investing and corporate social responsibility endorsed by numerous foundations and companies; and the exploding field of sustainable and green development promoted by environmentalists, urbanists, business leaders, academics, local governments, think tanks such as the Rocky Mountain Institute and Worldwatch Institute, and countless books with titles like *Capitalism at the Crossroads* (Stuart Hart), *Capitalism As If the World Matters* (Jonathon Porritt), and *Green to Gold* (Daniel Esty). BP is now "beyond petroleum" (yes, the jury's still out) and Wal-Mart's gone green (ditto); Al Gore's documentary wins the Academy Award while socially responsible investing grows; and sustainability studies have gained a toehold in policy institutes, governments, foundations, and higher education where, across a handful of disciplines, universities are training your town's future planners, economists, cultural leaders, educators, and corporate executives. According to business writer Andrew Savitz, "A generation of people in search of deeper meaning in their lives is now taking over the corporate suites." There's that little word again—*meaning*—and it's toward that word, even against formidable political and corporate pressures shoving against it, that sound economic policy has been drifting for at least half a century. Environmental historian Roderick Nash might describe the drift as the logical extension of an ethical eco-evolution, a process Leopold recognized as "an evolutionary possibility and an ecological necessity." This reappraisal of rights and responsibilities has led to social, moral, and governmental reforms deeply grounded in the principle that sense of place *does* matter, and that the ingredients of place are not only complex and interrelated but threatened. Leopold felt it on a mountain, today we see it on Main Street.

That's the direction the river is flowing, and it's time tourism quit rowing upstream toward a meaningless, dimensionless landscape. Weighing the consequences of not embracing the triple bottom line against the benefits of doing so, your local tourism team should find it easy to be on the right side of this question. Ask: What industry is better served than tourism by a clean, exhilarating, distinctive environment, both natural and built? Conversely, there probably isn't an economic sector more disadvantaged by a spoiled landscape, polluted air, drab buildings, and unsafe, anonymous sprawl. "Almost no other industry," writes David Edgell, "is as environmentally dependent as the tourism industry." And what commercial cluster is more socially dependent than tourism—benefiting from healthy interactions, suffering from weak ones? Because other businesses are defined predominantly by products that use, pollute, and waste, or by gizmos and services that can be outsourced, they must radically reinvent themselves to make the river trip toward "place" and "meaning," but a healthy tourism economy has always stood at that experiential nexus, so put the oars up and go with the flow, one that will carry you away from the false country built by machines, toward an authentic place where tourism *belongs*.

## *Concept or Culture*

I can imagine what some are thinking: But wait, for decades travel officials have talked about creating "win-win" partnerships with museums, parks, cultural agencies, and other members of the place society. I did the same for years, and today it's nearly impossible to attend a hospitality or economic development conference and not find a speaker canonizing some breed of place-based tourism because, as the popular melody goes, these travelers "stay longer and spend more." Or check your commerce department's website, and I wager you'll find language about "creative," "arts-driven," "heritage" or "sustainable" development as a key component of your state's tourism or overall "smart growth" campaign. Similarly, it's a rare travel bureau that doesn't manage or at least participate in a cultural heritage or ecotourism program, described in sophisticated websites and lush publications. And if you pick through the brochure rack at almost any chamber of commerce you'll likely come across a visitors guide with a picture of the local museum or a natural wonder on the cover, while inside you'll find a story about indigenous peoples, a trail or park system map, and a guide to art galleries and historic districts, all accompanied by a sketch of the area's past, an anecdote about a founding family, or a feature commemorating a historical event. We're light-years beyond the days when the only visitor handout was a motel map and list of restaurants, with good reason: as advertisers know, narrative sells, and more and more today the travel narrative is written from cultural and, increasingly, multicultural perspectives. That is all to the good.

But, and this is a big *but*, one that should preface all "sustainable," "green," "heritage," and "healthy" economic initiatives: Are we culturalizing commerce or commercializing culture? Who's doing the wagging, the dog or the tail? Are these trendy projects genuine or just more "sustainababble" and "greenwashing"? Richard Florida and others have breathed life back into creative economic policies (this is not the first go-round), but don't you get just a wee bit suspicious when your city's smart growth campaign is spearheaded by the housing industry?

Or when the department of commerce draws up sustainability plans? Serious "rethinking" of economic policy, especially if you intend to *act* on that policy, requires equally serious restructuring of decision-making systems. From top down consider: If "place" is so important to twenty-first-century economics, why is it being paved over at an alarming tempo? If "sense of place" is so vital to economic development, why has funding for culture, historic preservation, and environmental protection dipped at many levels this past decade? If "place-based tourism" is so grand, why haven't the promises made and dreams imagined years ago been fulfilled? Most haven't—just check your museum's budget and attendance figures. Clank. If it's such a "win-win," please explain how both ends of that equation share in the victory.

"Sense of place," we are told at most hospitality conferences, is central to the success of local tourism programs. In the eyes of some, however, the industry has become one of place's most feared predators, because the agencies which oversee local tourism planning are often the same ones that nurture or at least give safe harbor to a growth mania that continues to bulldoze your hillsides, suck life out of your downtown, tear apart the connective tissue of your public space, and bury your region's distinctive stories beneath a Jiffy Lube world of bland "Towne Centres" (usually an "e" on *town* and *center* the British way), office parks (always a lovely "park"), and Edge Cities that are named, says Joel Garreau in his book of the same title, after the very things they displaced: Quailwood has neither, anymore. Fox Meadows are gone, too. Both of them. And nothing creates sense of place like a cluster of windowless, boxy concrete slabs designed to last twenty years, wrapped in an ocean of treeless macadam, reachable only by a choked six-lane highway. Why is tourism development sometimes under the thumb of, or at least shaking hands with, that corrosive ethic? Considering the possibilities, it should be easy to walk away.

Similarly, economic development policy wonks who parrot Richard Florida and other captains of the New Economy write and talk about the importance of street culture and local heritage. But when they act on that conviction within a tourism context, because the economic bottom line has "a tendency to subvert and subjugate other considerations, ethical and environmental," argue Mowforth and Munt, the planners are sometimes complicit in converting authentic towns into plastic fairytales. What's with the ersatz Alpine villages in places where the only thing that's ever been Swiss is cheese or knives? Or communities marketed as "New Urbanist" because they added a faux Main Street crammed with the usual mall franchises. Can you say "façadomy"? It's not enough that these fake hamlets attract shutterbugs and turn a buck, as the propagandists argue—so might a Burger King on a Hopi mesa or Georgia's Kennesaw Mountain. Sure, that's a ridiculous comparison, but that's precisely the conversation you should be having, and citizens have every right to value their town as a reservation or national park—that is, as sacred space. Compromising your historic integrity and natural resources is not just bad for interpretation and preservation—it's bad for local businesses. Check Application 2.2 and compare the economic standings of places that preserve the environment, both built and natural, against those that don't. Case closed.

Because of the way place-based initiatives are often structured, and because of the growth priorities that underpin the structures, even when tourism and economic development agencies attempt "win-win" projects with the place sector the reality is there's too much "win-lose," and we know who's on the losing end: your community's identity, its character, its soul, its cultural narrative as well as the institutions that preserve and perpetuate that narrative. Simply put, current structures, priorities, and procedures lead travel programs to interpret "place" as little more than an economic "concept," rather than a necessary part of local "culture"—*and* the tourism agency's own culture. In his essay, "An Argument for Diversity," Wendell Berry explains the difference: "As a nation, we have attempted to substitute the *concept* of 'land use,' 'agri-business,' 'development,' and the like for the *culture* of stewardship and husbandry." A Kentucky farmer and poet, Berry is speaking about land management, but peach farmer Masumoto has already reminded us that tourism development could be farming's doppelganger: we plant, harvest, and sustain—all of it conditioned by what Donald Worster calls "values in the soil." Local tourism conversations could benefit immensely from Berry's agricultural ethic, which stresses a love of and respect for those land values and the community they sustain—in other words, operating from a *culture* of stewardship, Leopold's ethic. As a practical exercise, tourism programs might adapt the Asilomar Declaration for sustainable agriculture which, alongside other local farming initiatives, is committed to "hastening the broad adoption of an agriculture that is ecologically sound, economically viable, fair, and humane." To see how you might shift hospitality operations toward a culture of stewardship, read the Asilomar principles, and wherever they say "agriculture" substitute "tourism."

Sadly, some place-based tourism still operates as a concept, the equivalent of factory farming, producing plastic fruit instead of juicy peaches. Tourism programs continue to create more standardized products, technological gimmicks, fancy terminologies, beautiful publications, economic incentives, and trendy schemes to study, package, and promote alternative travel, but we have not developed a tourism culture that truly values place for itself. As a result, "When one of the non-economic categories is threatened," writes Aldo Leopold, "we invent subterfuges to give it economic importance"—forced to package our mountains and cultures within financial justifications, as if they are unworthy of preservation for their own sake. Without naming names here, the distressing result of "subterfuge thought," especially when it dictates tourism policy, is that some place-centric programs, not unlike agribusiness, favor mass marketing at the expense of product, use at the expense of preservation, entertainment at the expense of education, the shallow at the expense of the deep and authentic—all of it undermining legitimate natural, cultural, and historic resources *and* a more robust and sustainable economic return. The best one can say about some of these practices is they're neglectful, the worst is they're exploitative of or even harmful to place: "They erase the very history they claim to admire," laments Lucy Lippard. Still others damage social networks and the industry's reputation, such as bus tours through a drowned city. Imagine how those tours could have worked, in concert with and supportive of the community. That's civic tourism.

## Possibility Unbound: The Sweet Spot

In *Natural Capitalism: Creating the Next Industrial Revolution*, the authors begin their inquiry into a new, restorative economic design:

> Capitalism, as practiced, is a financially profitable, nonsustainable aberration in human development. What might be called "industrial capitalism" does not fully conform to its own accounting principles. It liquidates its capital and calls it income. It neglects to assign any value to the largest stocks of capital it employs— the natural resources and living systems, as well as the social and cultural systems that are the basis of human capital.

Rethinking economics so as to "assign . . . value" to natural and social markets, in addition to *the* marketplace, is the basis of triple-bottom-line accounting, the essence of the "creative" approaches proffered by New Economists. Sense of place, in all of its dimensions and permutations, matters to economic development. Some projects, it seems, want to cherry-pick their way through today's trendy analyses, figuring they can give public relations lip service to the language about historic streetscapes, cultural diversity, distinctive neighborhoods, a varied job base, wholesome environments, good schools and libraries, and other *quality* ingredients, and still come out ahead on the *quantitative* economic growth index. Others believe that if they stoke the financial churning first, the place stuff will follow. It probably won't.

Attracting and retaining high-value jobs that undergird the New Economy demands a genuine commitment to "place-making," a term coined by noted nineteenth-century landscape architect "Capability" Brown, and tourism is perfectly situated to serve that commitment. No other industry connects to the values of triple-bottom-line planning in such meaningful and functional ways. In your town, it's unlikely few other industries can contribute as much to or benefit as much from a healthy triple bottom line. Cities like Nashville, Boise, and Portland know and promote that, as do regional associations such as the Sierra Business Council in northern California or Pennsylvania's Lackawanna County. At an even broader level states like Michigan are employing alternative tourism to shed their industrial image. But few economic truth-tellers have recognized the possibility, and the hospitality sector has not called their attention to it. It's time to do so, not only in books like this one that toss about theory, but with action, situating tourism in the Venn diagram's sweet spot where *three* bottom lines intersect, not isolating it in the lonely financial sphere.

Situated thusly, at the base of Leopold's mountain, local tourism actors should protest the dismantling of their community's social ecosystem instead of abetting it. In addition to testifying on behalf of bills favorable to the airline or rental car industries, for instance, tourism officials should do the same for environmental protection, cultural preservation, and education. They should stand shoulder to shoulder with land trusts, conservancy programs, and environmental justice initiatives safeguarding both open and urban space, and they should respond to the "jobs or environment" shibboleth with facts. They should condemn the malling and billboarding and paving of landscapes by encouraging growth boundaries and sensible planning. They should partner with urbanists and preservationists to advocate for distinctive downtowns—pedestrian-friendly places designed around people, not more car-worshipping sprawl. Tourism agencies should not be reluctant to list their name alongside activist groups working to clean our air and streams, preserve our mountains and deserts, reduce waste and energy use, and save family farms from the crushing combine of agribusiness. They should support political and industry platforms that reward conservation and penalize wasteful practices, the reverse of today's code. They should stand up for local business rather than blindly invite more transnational franchises. They should help museums, art guilds, parks, and historic-preservation agencies protect and grow their dwindling budgets, and partner with these organizations to educate the public about regional heritage, including speaking out for more history in schools. Tourism programs should not shy away from lending their name to social programs: food banks, homeless shelters, affordable housing projects, leadership initiatives. They should be on the side of place, and their voices should support candidates who share that conviction.

From that perspective tourism stakeholders should work with universities, governments, and economic development agencies to lobby for and craft "creative" policies that benefit both the travel industry and the community—policies that attract high-value businesses, not those that simply want a bigger tax incentive; policies that move towns along the path toward a quality workforce, not merely "more jobs." With these missions and successes in the industry's back pocket, tourism publications, websites, and other communication tools, in addition to featuring glitzy graphs measuring overnight stays and taxes generated, should point out and celebrate these place-enhancing stories, demonstrating to citizens how "tourism planning as community planning" is protecting their region's distinctive legacies and wonders, how the industry is helping to secure well-paying jobs, and how a "rethought" economic policy, one responsive to local voices and values, is preserving and enhancing the community character that drew people there in the first place.

The growth machine has deep-pocketed lobbyists and corporations to do its bidding; many of the groups just mentioned don't, yet they are the ones that work to sustain your finest, most enduring, and arguably most profitable tourism attraction—a healthy sense of place. Scan the sales literature distributed by developers and note the pages filled with glossy pictures of forests and historic buildings; it's clear the machine also needs and exploits sense of place, as well as the tourism industry that promotes it. But that need is not mutual. In the end local hospitality initiatives will benefit more, and benefit their community more, by aligning themselves with those working to improve your region's social, cultural, and natural character, rather than by remaining in bed with asphalt companies that want to pave it over. Cared for well, that character will provide a better quality of life for residents and guests, and simultaneously fashion a more dynamic and sustainable economic base. Creating a healthy place touristically, a "community of character," just might land you that Google office.

A twofer and a nice wish list. Fat chance much of this will happen, though, unless communities retool tourism's decision-making structures and procedures, unless residents develop the political will to reframe what just might be their largest and loudest industry.

# *"Rethink Economics": Conversation Starters*

1. **Growth:** Is there a public sense of tourism's role related to growth and development? Does your community's tourism development plan operate under an "either/or" or "both/and" ethic? Would you say the paradigm primarily supports the "facilitator economy" or heritage-based projects that provide the tourism experience? What's the answer when you ask the Big Question: "*Why* do we do tourism?"

2. **New Economics:** Do the agencies that oversee economic development in your region use "creative" language in their presentations and publications? Are they aware of trends like the New Economy, and does there seem to be a regional movement to adopt such policies? If not, why? If so, how might tourism fit into the scheme?

3. **Concept:** If your community practices cultural tourism, heritage tourism, ecotourism, or some other form of place-based tourism, would you say the agencies that manage these programs operate from "concept" or "culture"? Have your museums and other heritage sites benefited from the tourism projects? Do they have a voice in the planning?

4. **Book Discussion Idea:** *The Rise of the Creative Class: And How It's Transforming Work, Leisure, Community and Everyday Life*, Richard Florida (2002). Agree with Florida or not, there's no doubt his book transformed the way some people look at economic development in the twenty-first century. Apply Florida's "creative" concepts to tourism development in your region.

# 3. CONNECT TO THE PUBLIC:
## *A Society To Match Our Scenery*

*Here were citizens reaffirming a small measure of control over their shared physical surroundings, and demonstrating a sense of community, which is part of what cities are about—or should be.* ~Witold Rybczynski, *City Life*

Predictably, hospitality's affair with the growth machine can drive an ugly wedge between the industry and those residents who complain, "tourism ruined my town," a not uncommon rant in communities where the industry has achieved economic linchpin status. We know these places, called "tourist traps" for a reason, and few of us want to live in them, but astonishingly wannabe tourism towns often hold them up as the machinery to model. As a result, some regions remain stuck in "capitalism's squirrel cage," to borrow economist Juliet Schor's fitting metaphor, trapped by and addicted to the tail-chasing policies that give rise to these plastic enclaves—boutique towns where you can buy a rubber tomahawk or a refrigerator magnet with a portrait of Jesus on it, but not a pair of brown socks. Your town might not be there yet, although pressures may be pushing in that direction, and hospitality executives who refuse to acknowledge and plan for the possibility of that unpleasant tipping point—when a place ceases to exist for itself or its residents—only to yammer on about jobs created or bed taxes generated, are neglecting their responsibility to the community and, ultimately, to their profession, turning tourism into a four-letter word among locals, spawning a palpable us-and-them rancor between residents and visitors, alienating the very taxpayers and voters the travel sector depends on. How can any of this be good for your hospitality agenda? How can you even think of fostering a constructive dialog about the future of tourism in your town, not to mention generate grassroots political support, when those who care at all remain dug in on opposite sides of a very high, thick wall?

The long list of scholars who study the history of the often troubled marriage between tourism and place, such as those represented in the recent anthology, *The Culture of Tourism, The Tourism of Culture*, remind us that there's little new in my complaint. We have always marketed "place" to spur visitation, whether it's Niagara Falls or the Grand Canyon, and, as was true with those two locations, we often bowdlerize, pasteurize, and bastardize some of the ingredients of place in the process, *and* incite the local community. In their formative visitation years both the Falls and the Canyon became so cluttered with tacky enterprises, tasteless development that obscured the very attraction, that public pressure eventually compelled the authorities to sweep away the commercial litter. Unfortunately, most towns don't enjoy that level of protection or public oversight and, as a result, the misapplication of place for travel has grown exceedingly more pervasive, because more communities have joined the tourism caravan, and "place" is their best and perhaps only product; because the financial incentives are alluring, given the high-value status of experiential travelers, at the same time the cash flow is more critical to local coffers; because few programs adequately explain how to fuse place and tourism; and, significantly, because there is often no one the hospitality industry answers *to*.

That last part is changing and civic tourism, which stresses public discussion of and local control over the travel agenda, represents one type of change, while elsewhere environmentalists, social activists, and governments are creating monitoring systems to report abuses, as well as to encourage and reward successes. Early activities have focused on ecotourism, such as the print and web-based travel guides that assess the legitimacy of nature-tour destinations. Eco-labeling of products, which has existed since the late 1970s, has reached into tourism as well, including the EU's probable eco-label for hotels. Before long similar monitoring and accrediting systems for cultural and heritage tourism programs may be commonplace. Already, for example, the increasing numbers of socially conscious travelers wishing to buy gifts from local artisans, lodge in establishments that pay a living wage, or otherwise leave a negligible social or ecological footprint can research their travel options online at Sustainable Traveler International, Green Globe's Travel Planner, and other services. Informed oversight is coming from the outside, but you need it on Main Street too, if only to avoid an avenue full of neon wedding chapels that obscure *your* Niagara Falls.

### Pride in Place and Profession

The historian and novelist Wallace Stegner once challenged us to "create a society to match [our] scenery." That's what "the poetry and politics of place" is about. Many communities already have the poetry, rooted in the compelling narratives of territories, towns, and traditions—the "scenery" Stegner reveres. Look beyond the crap of modernism and most places, in fact, have good bones, and if you squint your eyes and tilt your head slightly, it's not hard to imagine how the rhythms of that "poetry" might reveal themselves. These assets may never transform your town into Las Vegas, Branson, or Hilton Head, but cared for well they will help build a sustainable economy and a healthy quality of life, and do you really want to be those other places? If that's what success looks like for your town, you're reading the wrong book. Taking up Stegner's challenge, the other crucial and often neglected task is to create a society—that is, to design a "politics of place," a *citizen* politics that is the equal to your remarkable cultural and natural poetry. "Civic engagement and community process," writes Roberta Brandes Grantz, "are much more important to the long-term success of places than either the architect who designs or the developer who builds them."

Many helpful civic engagement guides and public participation manuals explain the mechanics of that process; but beyond the designs and procedures, especially when the topic is place-based tourism, one element distinguishes the towns that work from those that struggle: At its core this process must be grounded in a sense of pride in both place and the profession that sells our place to the world. Rightfully so, many of us spend a lot of time talking about pride in place—landscapes, cultures, downtowns, arts—and I want to travel a bit of that territory, especially the question, "What prompts pride in place?" What makes people care? Place doesn't just happen, and creating a mutual concern for it is even more elusive. It's not something mandated or legislated: "Hey you, be proud!"

Believing that pride in one's community is the first step toward a full-bodied conception of "citizenship," Daniel Kemmis urges us to rekindle the affection Athenians felt for their city, as expressed in Pericles's famous oration: "I would have you day by day fix your eyes upon the greatness of Athens, until you become filled with the love of her." Imagine how that devotion and commitment if expressed by, say, gas station attendants and retail clerks, not to mention elected officials and city planners, could begin to transform your community's hospitality program. Unfortunately, the origins of this level of care for and attachment to place are too little understood or cultivated today, but one note rings clear: The more people know the story of a place, the more likely they are to take pride in and be stewards of that place. Consequently, fostering a responsible place-based tourism ethic is made more practicable when you create additional opportunities to educate the public, including employees in the hospitality sector, about local history and culture. Innovative tourism training programs are doing just that— partnering with schools and heritage institutions to instill a sense of community pride in front-line staff, the people guests usually meet first. Museums can supplement these efforts by hosting open houses and receptions for travel industry employees, and they can lure in the public by thinking beyond their walls. For instance, to reach new residents museums might sponsor an updated version of Welcome Wagon, that instead of a fruit basket provides a video or book about local history—a way of saying, "Welcome, this is why we care."

Unjustifiably, if pride in the tourism profession is expressed at all, it's usually dressed in economic garb—trotted out in rose-tinted, jazzy PowerPoint pie charts that tally "heads in beds" and tchotchkes sold. What should *also* be implanted and valued, which is certainly doable at local and regional levels, where this conversation needs to take root, is that people who work in the tourism profession, whether motel clerks, museum directors, restaurateurs, or CVB officials, are in the business of sharing their home with strangers. What a noble profession, something one *should* take pride in, but sadly one seldom sees that sentiment expressed, let alone championed, at hospitality get-togethers. I'm still waiting to attend the travel conference where the P word is the theme of the three-day meeting,

APPLICATION 3.2

APPLICATION 1.3

where "Pride" hangs from banners and industry keynoters celebrate how tourism is helping to make our communities better places for residents, rather than the chest-thumping that occurs because your town went from a 4.3 to a 4.5 market share. What if, to achieve that .2 increase, you lopped off the top of a mountain to build a new hotel, a mountain revered by locals? A mountain gone forever. When I pointed this out to one city employee whose town had done something similar, the response was, "Well, I have a job." As Halstead, Rowe, and Cobb explain, that .2 means little, and its rah-rah interpretation is at best deceptive, absent other contexts: "The GDP is simply a gross measurement of market activity, of money changing hands. It makes no distinction whatsoever between the desirable and the undesirable, or cost and gain." In the place-making business, *and* the tourism business, "desirable" is a function of a robust triple bottom line, not simply the column that calculates GDP.

To help thwart the misuse of your area's land and heritage, in order to honor and benefit the people who live there *and* to design a high-value tourism strategy, it's important from the start to recognize the intrinsic humanistic nature of place, and then make its application indispensable to community conversations. Doing so can't help but raise a few basic and at times uncomfortable questions that test the way your area "does" tourism. So if, let's say, historic Main Street is your principal attraction, why isn't the tourism committee headquartered with the historical society or a preservation agency instead of the chamber of commerce, a city economic development department, or a marketing firm? If rivers, mountains, wetlands, wildlife, and open space are your product, why doesn't the parks division or an association of environmental groups manage tourism? Why does the convention and visitors bureau promote your town's cultural and natural wonders but not invest in their development or maintenance? In other words, why does economic development and advertising always trump product?

Absent systemic changes that realign priorities by, first, drawing the public into the conversations, larger political and organizational transformation—that is, moving from concept to culture—is unlikely for at least three reasons: First, much hospitality research, funding, and planning still flows from the top—from a state agency, for instance. Although tourism is vital to the economies of many small communities, few have the resources to carry out travel research, promotion, and product development without aide from above: state assistance programs whose funding is contingent on applicants meeting standardized benchmarks. Given this top-down architecture, one shaped by conformity, compartmentalization, limited resources, political expediency, and internecine turf battles, it generally turns out to be more efficient and cost-effective for state offices to encourage brands, images, or niches, rather than messy individual stories, and brands are nothing if not marketing concepts.

This rant is not about finger pointing or blaming state tourism offices, most of which do a lot with a little, and let's face it: place-making is not their mission. However, because of the tremendous economic, social, and environmental consequences that follow in the wake of today's expanding hospitality industry a new structure and expanded mission are called for. Given political realities and the lethargy of large bureaucracies, encouragement will have to come from the grassroots, from citizens who appreciate the possibility of a responsible place-based tourism ethic in their region. That means getting political, which requires rolling up your sleeves and getting your nails dirty. Right now there are well-funded mouthpieces at the legislature working *against* the qualities of place you hold dear. Citizens have a right, even an obligation, to speak *for* those qualities, and placed-based tourism is an appropriate preservation and economic development context in which to frame your argument.

Ultimately, in order for towns to practice tourism effectively and responsibly, they should speak in unison, encouraging states to invest far more in tourism development. However, rather than simply increase the state office's marketing budget, industry advocates at the local level should help grow and shape the program at the top so more resources flow directly to regional tourism programs for the needs specific to each place—a bottom-up individualized process, in other words, rather than top-down standardization. Tourism is simply too important and influential to be left to underfunded state bureaucracies and struggling local agencies—most of which, given their historical mandates and limited resources, view tourism development through a predictably narrow lens.

Second, even at the local level, as long as chambers of commerce, city departments of economic development, advertising agencies, and the traditional hospitality voices define and position "sense of place" for your region's tourism agenda, it's simply unfair to expect them, absent any other encouragement or resources, to do otherwise than conduct place-based tourism as a concept, since most staff are business and marketing professionals, not historians, cultural experts, or ecologists. About the "place" product, there is often a sense that "someone will do that." When chambers of commerce, for instance, undertake tourism R&D, it's usually to determine more effective advertising strategies, not to create better products. When they *do* speak of "product development," a fashionable phrase today among tourism officials, it generally means "indexing" and "repackaging" existing attractions—branding, itinerary building, and the like. It certainly doesn't mean allocating the chamber's inadequate resources to build new products or enhance what's already there. I certainly endorse marketing and support municipalities and legislatures appropriating more money for tourism promotion. We've seen the consequences of defunding advertising programs, such as Colorado's disastrous decision to eliminate its office of tourism. However, communities should recognize that marketing is but half the tourism equation, and they simply must invest in product development, both conceptually and financially, which also demands political mobilization.

A third reason we have not developed a culture of place-based tourism is that, as noted earlier, hospitality remains a young, evolving enterprise in many towns, and overlaying tourism's profit motive with the place sector's preservation ethic is an even more recent experiment. This is new stuff, and it's easy to become disillusioned and imagine the barriers are too high. Don't. A little historical perspective illustrates just how swiftly these developments have come upon us and, if we study our history, communities today can make more informed and effectual choices. In 1950, for instance, fewer than 25 million international travelers visited the United States, and today that number is close to one billion. Pause for a second, do the math, and absorb what those numbers mean, potentially, for the economy but also for social networks and environmental policies. Similarly, in 1950 fewer than 2,400 museums dotted the nation's landscape, while today there are more than 18,000. In many ways our hospitality industry and heritage community have grown up together, running along parallel tracks laid down by a post–World War II economic euphoria and the automobile, which together democratized travel and culture for many families who traditionally experienced neither. Those tracks merged a generation or so ago with the popularization of ecotourism, cultural tourism, and related models, but as other markets have shown, evolving from concept to culture takes time and the road is often rocky.

Consider almost any other extractive industry, whether lumbering, agriculture, fishing, or mining, and note how that history parallels tourism's. Especially in the late nineteenth and early twentieth centuries, when all but a handful of people such as George Marsh or John Muir considered America's natural resources inexhaustible, mining and other industries often set up shop with virtually no constraints, not unlike early tourism boosters at Niagara Falls. Government land agencies, in fact, were principally in the business of making minerals, land, and water available to industry, and Aldo Leopold and his fellow foresters were as much tree and game brokers as preservationists. Easy money followed for a few corporations, but in the process of heedlessly digging up or chopping down resources, local economies, landscapes, and societies suffered, and unless smarter methods were developed, such as Leopold's inspired work in the 1930s, or unless preservationists succeeded at cordoning off entire sections for parks and wilderness, the long-term prognosis for many land-based economies was exceedingly dim. Our landscape is pocked with evidence of those shattered dreams.

Critics say the tourism industry can trigger similar environmental, economic, and social collapse, a conviction that has given rise to sustainable tourism and similar designs. Being a recent economic player in many places, especially smaller towns, tourism has just begun to entertain these resource questions, mostly because the public has goaded the industry in that direction, not because the travel delegation has driven itself there. Tourism communities might take a page from the experiences of land-based economies, which, after decades of trial and error, have adopted more deliberative and collaborative planning approaches to potentially divisive issues, often mandated by regulations like the National Environmental Policy Act (NEPA, 1969). Elsewhere, creative initiatives such as the Forest Stewardship Council (FSC), now operating in more than sixty countries, bring citizens, governments, environmentalists, the timber industry, and retailers together to forge wood harvesting policies that sustain the economy, indigenous cultures, and the natural environment. Principle 6 of FSC's ten-point plan, for example, reads: "Forest management shall conserve biological diversity . . . and maintain the ecological functions and the integrity of the forest." If it's possible for people to discuss that contentious issue in a constructive manner, certainly cultural groups, land-use agencies, residents, and the hospitality sector can work together toward agreed-upon ends.

## A Third Seat at the Table

Few tourism policies today publicly question the desire to involve citizens. Yet, write Martin Mowforth and Ian Munt, "The debate is currently not one of whether local communities should be involved in the development of tourism to their areas, but how they should be involved and whether 'involvement' means 'control.'" Well, yes, it does. Whose place is it? Whose place is it when a swanky transnational lodging chain pays Kalahari Bushmen a few coins a day to stand in the hotel lobby in grass skirts and "look African"? Whose place is it when these outside investors modify the continent's deep-rooted people-land-animal dynamics? Whose place is it when the hotel corporation determines tourism policy, messes with local politics, and reaps most of the profit, which is sent packing to a European bank account? Ask the same question about your town. The Africans did, and policies are changing.

Absent local voices of influence and "control," planning can become insular and insensitive, operating in a vacuum where economic policy has gone unchallenged for too long, where place is rarely valued as something other than a tick in a spreadsheet column, where few remember that "steady state" is nature's norm and continued growth an aberration. To address that gap, a "civic" structure is needed, a more inclusive, equitable, accountable, and multidimensional approach that will go by different names in different towns, but one that will:

- **Restructure and relocate the policy-making paradigm.** Move the voice for place-based tourism development outside the chamber of commerce, city economic development agency, or related marketing culture. Create a new "civic" base for conversations. Because of their connection to "place," history museums are a particularly appropriate institution to house deliberations, but the committee should represent all community voices, including those from the traditional tourism sector.

- **Develop more creative, inclusive, and transparent procedures to evaluate place-based development.** Consult the civic engagement agencies and publications mentioned here, attend their trainings, and incorporate deliberative philosophies and methods into everyday operations. Make inclusivity standard procedure, not a tactic you roll out when it's convenient or politically expedient.

- **Privilege social and environmental bottom lines equitably against economic returns.** Study the values that define the New Economy and incorporate triple-bottom-line logic into tourism designs. Work with universities and economic development departments to recast tourism. Encourage public members, in particular, to monitor social and environmental indicators. Embed TBL philosophy into everything you do, not just selected operations, and recognize that the triple bottom line is conditioned and improved through civic engagement.

- **Encourage a broader understanding of and appreciation for local history and heritage.** As I argue elsewhere, the more people know a place, the more likely they are to take pride in that place, which is a helpful addition to any travel program. Conduct heritage trainings for hospitality employees, partner with cultural agencies on community activities, support increased funding for museums and heritage sites, and urge schools to teach more local history and culture so students learn early on to appreciate their community's story.

- **Imagine tourism as a necessary and responsible part of a larger social ecology.** Communities cannot afford to consider tourism distinct from other social, financial, and environmental ingredients of place. *All* tourism conversations should be conducted within ecological frameworks, not along a strictly linear and separate plane. From the other direction, city councils and planners should factor tourism into *their* deliberations. Tourism planning and town planning should be inseparable. Ecological thinking is inclusive, holistic, regional, and long-term.

- **Ground discussions and decisions in core values.** Ralph Waldo Emerson reminded us that values come first, technique second: "The man who grasps principles can successfully select his own methods. The man who tries methods, ignoring principles, is sure to have trouble." Find out what citizens care about and design tourism operations around those values and principles. What do people really connect to? What do they want to improve and sustain? How can a retooled tourism program respond to those desires? Let residents know how you are addressing their concerns through tourism.

That's a daunting if not impossible frame flip in some towns, I know, but one that's made slightly less impossible when you begin by broadening the dialog. I'm speaking here to historical societies, conservation groups, preservation programs, educators, leadership institutes, community activists, and tourism professionals concerned about the direction of their place. Don't expect traditional hospitality stakeholders, absent other incentives and pressures, to suddenly get religion and modify their mission from within. It's *not* a chicken-or-egg question: structural change at the local level must come first. I've heard museum directors, for instance, say their travel bureau designed a heritage tourism program and didn't include them in the planning. Well, don't wait to be invited; either invite yourself or set your own table, the recommendation here. And while chambers of commerce, CVBs, hotel associations, and city economic development agencies certainly warrant a seat at the table, you need many more chairs, for museum staff, park rangers, artists, preservationists, tribal voices, librarians, ministers, architects, and others representing cultural and heritage sectors—the "place" delegation.

I'm not saying much new here, of course, but in previous place-tourism partnerships, which toss around phrases like "win-win" and "shared vision," we've often come up short, one reason being that operations remain centered in agencies where the churning ethic dominates, such as city government or a chamber of commerce, the realm of "concept" not "culture." Also bottlenecking progress is that *within* the place and tourism sectors no single voice speaks for either, both groups comprised of dozens of players who don't even agree with one another. The hospitality sector, for example, is highly fragmented, including everything from a guy in a bathrobe, sitting in his basement designing a B&B's website, to the general manager of an international hotel chain. The place sector is equally disjointed—from a mom-and-pop museum to a national park. Another stumbling block is that even if the groups decide who speaks for whom, the missions and methodologies of the two sectors are so radically different that reaching common ground has traditionally proven elusive, resulting in a muddy middle that satisfies few. In fact, if we wanted to design two diametrically opposed groups to work together, we probably couldn't do much better than this:

| Tourism Community | Place Community |
|---|---|
| Private Businesses | Usually Nonprofit or Public |
| Commercial Goal | Educational Goal |
| Customer-centered (use) | Product-centered (conserve) |
| Funded by Exchange | Donations, Grants, Appropriations |
| Mass Market | Individualistic |
| Fast, Assembly Line | Slower, Reflection |
| Corporate, Distant Management | Local Oversight |
| Success = More, More, More! | Success = Value Added |
| Facilitates Experience | Provides Experience |
| Marketing | Product Development |
| Vocabulary: "Destination" | Vocabulary: "Place" |

Donald Worster's discussion of our nation's schizophrenic agricultural policy in *The Wealth of Nature* strikes a chord here:

> Furthermore, both science and agriculture must acknowledge that they cannot teach that awareness to each other. Such thinking must come from outside the relationship, from ethics and philosophy, from politics and social discourse, from the community at large trying to discover a new relationship to nature.

Consequently, if your community is serious about reaching "agreed-upon goals" or a "shared vision" for place-based tourism development, situate the conversation outside the conventional power spheres and, most importantly, involve the general public: those who know and care about place, who are often on the receiving end of tourism decisions, who function as a broker between the tourism and place sectors—and in so doing shift the conversation from mechanics to values. That's a particularly apt and useful process where place-based tourism is concerned because "place" is nothing if not a values-centric, humanistic principle with which people identify.

Significantly, "visions" and "shared goals" and "common ground" begin in and are a product of core values, which, when shared, lead to opinions and finally to action. Working outward from core values is a fitting role for the public to play here because most citizens aren't "experts" in tourism development or cultural programming, and unlike the professionals they don't get bogged down in procedures, jargon, technicalities, and system-speak. Nor are they as concerned with protecting political or programmatic turf, which is too often the case with tourism and heritage stakeholders. Citizens know what they care about and value; the question is, "How can a responsible tourism ethic get them there?" In *Coming to Public Judgment*, Daniel Yankelovich describes that very conversation, moving toward solutions only after shared values have been identified: "When the issue is presented to the public, it is the value side that must be accentuated and the technical side deemphasized, with the understanding that once the value questions are settled the issue can be safely returned to the experts." When the local tourism conversation is entered through that door, the process can actually help foster something that's sorely lacking today, something that, more than any best practice or business model, provides the blueprint for citizen-driven tourism: civil society.

### Out of Our Boxes

David Mathews writes that John Maverick's likely seventeenth-century comment about a New England village's local dispute—"We have a problem, let's talk about it"—should "go down in history as the quintessential American political speech," because Maverick's proposed solution heralded the beginnings of the town meeting, a logical extension of Enlightenment philosophies and an important step in securing the "exceptionalism" characteristic of American democracy. Indeed, if the idea of civil society achieved its most insightful expression in Europe, the more authentic model was realized in America, but while Thomas Jefferson's notion of "little republics," where citizens come together to discuss tough issues, is the idea upon which our country was founded, anyone who's worked in the political arena knows how difficult civic engagement can be. On one hand, people just don't show up. Even Richard Florida agrees there's a disturbing undercurrent to the chic set: "The leading force for political change, the creative class, has for all intents and purposes opted out of the political process." Whether it's apathy, busy schedules, television, or the feeling that their voice (or vote) doesn't matter, the public's withdrawal from many things associational has been well documented, sometimes referred to as the "bowling alone" syndrome. Linking "sense of place" and "social capital," urbanist Andres Duany believes our bland patterns of place may contribute to the erosion of social ties: "It is worth investigating the significant role that our changing physical environment may play in that perceived decline." On the other hand, when citizens do participate in city council meetings or public hearings, little *hearing* actually occurs—the process devolving into caustic debate, stonewalling, and grandstanding, rather than a deliberative search for that mysterious common ground.

Rarely mentioned in the literature on engagement, the tourism industry is the poster child for some of the civic problems scholars and activists study, one reason being that hospitality is defined by transience, an acknowledged impediment to communitarian values—with tourists coming and going, of course, but also persistent mobility within the profession. Attend a meeting about your city parks or library, for example, and note how few voices represent the travel sector, even though it may be among the area's leading economic drivers. There *are* wonderful exceptions, civic-minded tourism professionals, many I've worked with, but it's telling that they're thought of as exceptions. Setting them aside, tourism operations tend to rate on the engagement meter as either (1) no engagement: the hospitality sector does not listen to residents, and the public has little interest in tourism; (2) bogus engagement: the tourism bureau sponsors events in the name of "participation," but they're little more than public relations charades, such as conducting focus groups whose findings are predetermined, or sponsoring a meeting where a member of the agency's speakers bureau simply extols hospitality's economic benefits; (3) nasty engagement: meetings that degenerate into chamber of commerce boosterism versus environmentalists' protectionism.

To embark upon the journey toward a *shared* tourism ethic communities should do more than restructure the decision-making organization and invite other people to the party. They must focus on the *process* of productive engagement, which is more than salesmanship, focus groups, or talking at people. It's also not easy, so challenging that some tourism organizations invent excuses not to step into the waters: We're too busy, it's not our mission, people just want to complain, and we're the tourism experts anyway. Practical guides and prototypes do exist, such as community tourism, Ireland's rural tourism councils, Italy's citizen-based approach to farm tourism, and imaginative experiments in Australia and several African nations. What's missing from this picture? Unfortunately, for most conventional programs in the US the tourism-public dynamic is similar to the disconnect between hospitality and the New Economy—an awkward handshake at best, although the potential is considerable.

Of all employment sectors tourism is one of the most social, in that relations with both residents and guests are critical to the industry's long-term success. "Few large industries evoke such close, face-to-face contact," notes Erve Chambers. But while many tourism programs have improved *customer* relations, most local operations pay scant attention to residents, the people often most affected by the industry's decisions, cautioned Peter Murphy more than twenty years ago: "It is the citizen who must live with the cumulative outcome of such developments and needs to have greater input into how his community is packaged and sold as a tourist product on the world market." And while some travel officials, practitioners, and planners heed Murphy's advice and *say* to involve the public, few explain *how* to do it, and the process is key. Elsewhere it's a lot of window dressing and PR rhetoric. Correspondingly, even less attention is paid to the travel sector by civic engagement scholars and organizations. Whereas historians and sociologists have studied the industry's corporate culture and visitor habits and demographics for decades, one seldom reads a study about citizen participation or attends a conference on community building that even mentions tourism—again, one of the world's largest economic sectors; an influential actor that can shape built, natural, and cultural landscapes; and an undeniably socially embedded industry.

To remedy this lag, civic tourism sponsors workshops that urge local planning committees to draw on more than fifty years of research on and practice with public engagement, much of it aimed at pulling people out of their boxes, stressing "both/and" solutions (in our case: both tourism *and* a healthy place) instead of hackneyed "either/or" paradigms (either a healthy place *or* a tourism economy). Other models are readily available and adaptable, including Study Circles and the Kettering Foundation's National Issues Forum, which provide direction and resources for implementing productive meetings (your library may circulate these materials). Further, colleges and universities offer courses on citizen participation, often housed in nonprofit leadership schools. Associations such as Partners for Livable Communities, National League of Cities, Pew Partnership for Civic Change, and International Association for Public Participation host workshops, while OneWorld.net, WorldCafe.com, and other online ventures promote civil society in the blogosphere. At the very least consider incorporating their techniques into your strategy sessions and public outreach. Finally, newsletters, journals, and books, including Robert Putnam's best-selling (and controversial) publications on social capital, regularly roll off the presses, advice that should find its way onto your bookshelf and into your planning. If we're going to think of the tourism industry as a responsible corporate citizen, with both rights and responsibilities, that means stepping out of our comfort zones and engaging the community in local forums on its terms. That will take time and training because many tourism operations see themselves as marketing agencies, and engagement is marketing's mirror opposite.

In addition to the Forest Stewardship Council and NEPA models mentioned earlier, tourism conversations can also benefit from the experiences of other sectors that have embraced public participation, including government, education, land use, social services, and journalism. Tourism leaders can study the evolution of movements such as public journalism, for example, to learn from its successes and avoid the pitfalls. Other helpful models include the business-activist-community partnerships that operate today under the "sustainable development" rubric, where former combatants like BP Oil and Greenpeace are forging alliances. As the coauthors of *Walking the Talk* write,

> Many NGOs recognize that they cannot ignore the market if they want to find and deliver solutions to complex environmental and social problems. These organizations may believe that the private sector and the market cause many of those very same problems, but a number of them realize that for that very reason these institutions are part of the solution.

That's a hint to environmentalists, preservationists, and no-growthers, whose entrenched opposition to tourism contains a built-in Catch-22: If they succeed at creating lovely "livable places," then people, that is, *tourists*, are going to want to visit! Rather than perpetuate the age-old antagonistic frame, these groups should get out in front and partner with the hospitality sector, helping to reshape what we mean by "tourism," and creating a vision for the industry that benefits residents as much as visitors—creating a vision, in fact, for a new political paradigm, as Mathews characterizes it: "Conventional politics stresses the need for leaders who will create 'solutions.' Citizen politics stresses the importance of citizens claiming their own responsibility and becoming solutions themselves."

The point is, there's no dearth of resources, templates, consultants, or practical information to help communities expand and enrich the tourism conversation, but with the exception of a few bright lights, including those noted above or the National Park Service's work with gateway communities, the tourism sector generally has shied away from deliberative planning techniques that respond to voices outside the industry's traditional stakeholders. Most creative engagement activities that *do* take place are found in other countries, while in the US tourism-place-public collaborations are still considered pioneering, rather than standard procedure woven throughout all local operations. Equally troublesome, the "healthy," "sustainable," and "livable" communities networks, most of which incorporate civic engagement as a standard tool, as well as social activists who stress "civic organizing," have been all but silent about tourism, an industry that can seriously jeopardize or augment their place-saving goals.

Three tiny obstacles, it seems, stand in the way: the public, the planners, and the tourism industry, and here's a word for each. In this age of "bowling alone" it's often difficult to excite people about local issues, unless NIMBY rears its nasty head. The challenge is even greater for our discussion, since many citizens pay tourism little if any attention, regarding it as no more than a trivial low-wage industry—an amorphous collection of motels, franchise restaurants, signage, and T-shirt shops that often mark out those parts of town locals avoid. Tourism is more than that: Your museums, parks, historic districts, forests, libraries, and other community assets, like it or not, are in the "tourism business." Your home is for sale. So don't advertise a community meeting to discuss "tourism planning." Do the opposite. If we can get that message across to residents, perhaps tourism can be a partial antidote to the evaporation of civil society, especially the alternative versions of travel shaped by a community's sense of place—the cultural, social, and natural ingredients residents connect to, identify with, and care for. In *Policy Design for Democracy*, Schneider and Ingram lean toward that very possibility: "In terms of encouraging citizenship, a grassroots design that acknowledges the sense of place and the relevance of different cultures, histories, and experiences would seem to best engage the interests of citizens."

Elsewhere, colleagues and caretakers in the community-building network, as well as city managers and planners, especially New Economy evangelists, have asked why I concern myself so much with tourism, with trinket-shop politics: "Why aren't you tackling something 'important,' like immigration, the environment, or jobs?" Tourism, of course, connects to all three, often significantly, and as the industry continues to spread, which most studies forecast, it will become an even greater agent for change in our communities, intensifying its grip on all three of these "important" problems. Tourism obviously is not the most crucial issue in many places, but scholars, activists, practitioners, and public officials who work in economic development, smart growth campaigns, or the healthy communities arena, and who do not account for the hospitality industry in their financial, environmental, or social calculations, do so at their peril. Left to its own devices the tourism juggernaut can roll over years of hard work overnight, or the industry can be a valuable ally, a tool to help realize your vision. Don't you enjoy quality travel experiences? Why shouldn't all towns be afforded the opportunity to provide and benefit from that transaction?

A third challenge stems from the industry itself, which traditionally has stood outside the social ecology we call a community, not part of mountain thinking, willing to let other people, organizations, or city departments build its products and deal with its messes. Astonishingly, Goeldner and Ritchie can write, "The tourist industry cannot be held responsible for the occurrence of crimes." Rubbish, you're part of a community. Elsewhere, I've heard chamber of commerce directors and economic development officials say they don't want residents "anywhere near" their tourism operations, because the public either doesn't understand how the industry works or citizens only want to gripe. First, this is a values conversation, and just as people don't have to know the intricacies of a missile's calibrating system in order to form a moral position on war and defense, the public doesn't have to know the mechanics of tourism to form public judgment about its effects in their community. For some, it's an easy call—just look around. And that which they do need to know is your responsibility to communicate, as Jefferson said: "I know of no safe depository of the ultimate powers of society but the people themselves; and if we think them not enlightened enough to exercise their control with a wholesome discretion, the remedy is not to take it away from them, but to inform their discretion by education." Last, if residents complain, perhaps they have good cause, to which it's also your responsibility, as a corporate citizen and neighbor, to listen, respond, and possibly act. It's not your tourism program.

### Possibility Unbound: Civil Society

Successful alliances and genuine public engagement are distinguished by a *deliberative, transparent, responsible, and equitable* process that works toward building inclusive partnerships of trust—between and among businesses, the heritage sector, community caretakers, government, and the public. In fact, it is often the process that is more important than the product, the journey that is more important than the finish line, because that journey serves to build a foundation for civic leadership, above and beyond any tourism agenda. As Michael Briand writes in *Practical Politics*:

> No individual or group of individuals—no matter how talented, visionary, or exceptional—can do for the public what only the public in its entirety can and must do for itself. . . . We might say, then, that a leader is any citizen—any member of the public—who takes it upon himself or herself to enable and encourage his or her fellow citizens to bring their abilities, skills, and energies to bear on the task of forming a common perspective, reaching a shared judgment, and making a collective choice about what to do.

Just as tourism is a textbook tool to unlock the New Economy, if development priorities are rethought, so too is tourism perfectly suited to enable civil society, again, if we rethink the decision-making process. In both form (who gets to play) and methodology (how they play) this process is not the property of any single entity—neither the traditional hospitality sector, whose tenuous connection to place has historically been market-driven rather than asset-based, nor government agencies, given their inability to operate outside the lines. Civic tourism workshops, stacks of publications, and numerous citizen-engagement organizations can demonstrate the mechanics, but these are only tools—a compass, if you will, not the path itself. In more than a few ways, museums, historical societies, preservation groups, and land-use agencies, because of their deep-seated connection to both place and the public, are the institutions to lead citizens down the path toward a reframed tourism, to campaign for and spearhead a reorganized approach to product development, and to stimulate the conversation—in collaboration with those sectors of the hospitality community that value the tourism experience as a place-making tool, rather than an economic development card that trumps every other hand.

One hopes the values expressed by citizen initiatives eventually creep into all agencies and ventures that touch tourism, so the standing of "place" and the role of local voices are factored into every operation. In the end, a genuine "civic" tourism calls for a community-based approach that privileges the values expressed by the citizenry, not the economic priorities relished by a thin but influential slice of politically mobilized elites. With that process in place only then are you prepared to tackle the question that many hospitality operations jump to right out of the gate: What is our product?

# "Connect to the Public": Conversation Starters

1. **Perceptions:** What is the public's attitude toward tourism in the community? Among the general public, not tourism practitioners, is the industry appreciated and thought of as a good economic provider, or is it considered a tacky collection of minimum-wage jobs? Do citizens gripe about tourists in newspaper editorials and public meetings, or do they seem welcoming to visitors? Is there "tourism tension" in town, either because tourists have taken over and locals don't feel as if the town belongs to them, or because the industry has not delivered on its economic promises?

2. **Pride:** Do residents seem proud of your local history, culture, and natural wonders? If so, how is this pride expressed and shared with others, i.e., tourists? Have you ever attended a tourism planning meeting or read an annual report? If so, is the main conversation about the place or the profession? Where does pride reside for the tourism industry?

3. **Structure:** If your town were to develop a citizen-driven approach to tourism development, who might lead the reorganization (a person or agency)? What topical issue might give rise to this committee? Do you think the traditional tourism industry would welcome or balk at such an undertaking? Are there organizations in town from whom your committee can learn civic engagement procedures?

4. **Book Discussion Idea:** *Civic Innovation in America: Community Empowerment, Public Policy, and the Movement for Civic Renewal*, by Carmen Sirianni and Lewis Friedland (2001). Although this book is heavy on academics and never mentions tourism, the many examples provide models for other local engagement programs.

# 4. INVEST IN THE STORY:
## *Revealing the Genius of a Place*

*It was the Indian manner to vanish into the landscape, not to stand out against it.
...They seemed to have none of the European's desire to "master" nature, to arrange
and re-create. They spent their ingenuity in the other direction; in accommodating
themselves to the scene in which they found themselves.* ~Willa Cather, *Death Comes
for the Archbishop*

Who decided that your community should market itself to the world as a golfing
mecca or frontier-themed village? Who created the slogan beneath your town's
name on the sign that welcomes visitors? Who determined, because of your region's
magnificent mountains, that your community should position itself to attract
nature-based tourists—that you should join the swelling ranks of "green cities"?
Chances are those decisions were made by a fairly narrow sliver of the population,
or perhaps even a public relations firm hired to develop a brand—to build, in
other words, a "sense of place" through advertising. Civic tourism, conversely,
urges communities to invest in the story, to create a sense of place through product
development, a sometimes difficult and potentially disruptive undertaking because
doing so requires a strong *conceptual* and *financial* commitment to place-making,
and anytime ideas and money get mixed together, well. . . .

Place-making for touristic purposes is such a thorny proposition, in fact, that
if you look around your region or state and ask who's doing it, most likely the
answer is no one. Or the process is scattered across private and public agencies
at city, state, and federal levels; it's episodic at best, with capacity-building, staff
resources, and funding opportunities coming and going; rural communities are
usually hamstrung or simply out of luck; and the making of place, such as it is, often
has no direct connection to the hospitality industry. To invest in the story, then,
to address what is often the missing link in place-based tourism development,
your local citizen committee faces three tricky tasks: *uncover* this thing called
"place" in your region, *decide* if and possibly how place can be articulated for
tourism development, and *find resources* to preserve, improve, and maintain it.
That's all, get going.

Thankfully the hospitality sector today has room for people such as Becky
Anderson, the architect of HandMade in America (HMA), an amazing heritage
tourism program in North Carolina that is reviving regional economies at the
same time it helps citizens preserve their distinctive arts and traditions. HMA and
creative, citizen-centered ventures like it, such as geotourism, the Danish cultural
immersion programs known as life-seeing tourism, and activities worldwide
undertaken in the spirit of community tourism, provide localized models for

APPLICATION 4.3

regions struggling with place-making goals and procedures. The approach, which regards visitors as something other than "walking wallets," needn't be limited to rural Appalachia, Denmark, or a small island off Borneo. Bring it to Main Street. Specifically, invite guests into your story by having residents share their experience of and pride in place, a rendezvous of cultures, senses, and emotions that, significantly for tourism economies, prompts visitors to stay and return, triggers invaluable word-of-mouth advertising, and ultimately produces self-balancing systems: sense of place serves the tourism economy while appropriately designed travel activities reinforce the public's idea of place—an input-output scenario that defines a true "sustainable economy."

### "Uncover": All This Place Twaddle

This is where the possibility of local tourism begins, in providing guests a sense of what a place would look and feel like if they belonged there, giving them, says Neil Everden, "evidence of what has occurred there . . . the outside of what goes on inside"—the felt manifestation of a community's story, including the tourist's role in that story. That feeling of awe and attachment emerges almost effortlessly in some settings, such as a national park or a rural highway in central Montana, but how does your town manufacture a built counterpart? How do you induce visitors standin' on a corner in Winslow, Arizona, to feel as if they belong? *That* is what all the "sense of place" twaddle today should be about—not simply selling it, but listening *to* and providing visitors an authentic experience *of* the "genius of a place," as Alexander Pope famously expressed it. More than three hundred years later economist Richard Florida agrees, for pocketbook and social reasons: "Place is becoming the central organizing unit of our economy and society," an opinion seconded by other economists, New Urbanists, environmentalists, politicians, cultural practitioners, and city planners—and the word certainly has earned a lot of currency in hospitality circles.

Fine, but what do we mean by "place," especially when it's gift-wrapped for tourists' consumption? It's more than adding a picture of an old cowboy's rugged face, forest trail, or historic courthouse to a brochure. It's more than a brand. Anyone who's ever worked in a heritage site knows how difficult place-making can be—a process burdened with political, social, economic, cultural, and interpretive baggage, and no matter how hard you try, you'll probably offend, alienate, or otherwise disappoint someone. The question of "authenticity" alone, which I treat briefly in Application 4.2, fills museum studies publications and scholarly meetings, and yet it remains an imprecise concept that informed people continue to debate. As it should. Now take that same complex process and extend it to Main Street, which is essentially what place-based tourism does. It's not always an easy thing to do, which is why people and institutions associated with this work should be at the planning table, and it's also why travel programs designed around a community's story benefit from a robust *investment*: R&D for place, just as tourism's marketing agencies conduct ample research and development to determine and implement the best advertising strategies. Without doubt, place-making—interpreting and showcasing a region's story—is a topic that's debated endlessly in college classrooms, museum studies conferences, and urban planning laboratories. Practitioners spend decades figuring it out, so the few words here concentrate on uncovering the idea of place, as interpreted and expressed through ecological and organic filters (mountain thinking), and connecting that idea to the possibility of tourism. That is to say, what follows is necessarily fuzzy, not unlike the topic before us.

One thing is so: "place" is seldom a single attraction or point on the map. In the 1731 epistle quoted above, Pope hints that the experience of place results when "Parts answering parts will slide into a whole"—in other words, an *ecological* approach similar to the Eastern and Native American belief systems that helped shape Leopold's mountain thought: "Disease is a condition of division and separation from the harmony of the whole," writes Laguna Pueblo/Sioux author Paula Gunn Allen. "Beauty is wholeness. Health is wholeness. Goodness is wholeness." It's a view echoed by romantics such as Goethe ("Separateness is the illusion / One and many are the same"); Richard Florida and fellow urbanists ("Successful places are built up as complex, multifaceted ecosystems that, like those occurring in the natural world, defy simplistic linear thinking"); and Andres Edwards and other contemporary sustainability advocates ("By understanding the value of the relationships in an ecosystem rather than merely its components, we will be better positioned to make wise decisions").

Because the whole is more than the sum of its parts, those who study nature's ecosystems recognize *diversity* as a key to healthy "wholes" and "ones." Leopold, for example, said preserving "every cog and wheel is the first precaution of intelligent tinkering," earlier Charles Elton wrote of "the conservation of variety," and of course Rachel Carson's monumental *Silent Spring* is premised on safeguarding even the tiniest and most bothersome pests. The list goes on. Theirs is a biotic view that researchers and planners extend to economics, social networks, architecture, land use, and urban design: "variety and vitality," as city historian Witold Rybczynski describes it. Adopting and adapting this ecological machinery for tourism means encouraging a complex and evolving diversity, not a static sameness; many small players instead of a few large ones; a geography of differentiation in texture, form, and content; and a variety of relevant experiences rather than a single, often incompatible, tourist "acraption." The local tourism voice, to sum up, should speak on behalf of homegrown businesses, regional customs, historic appropriateness, and distinctive streetscapes, not a disconnected hegemony that undermines healthy ecosystems.

Fortunately, doing so is often easier and less costly than the alternative. As regional planner Benton MacKaye, the famed architect of the Appalachian Trail, wrote nearly fifty years ago, "place" rarely needs to be purpose-built—no new shopping centers, stadiums, or "attractions," many of which never return on their investment because the thinking is bass-ackward. Both the film *Roger & Me* and the book *The Tourist City* hold up the $100 million AutoWorld in Flint, Michigan, which closed in six months, as an example of build-big-stuff-and-they-will-come bonehead thinking. Perhaps your town, like many others, could write a book about hospitality's white elephants—gobs of money thrown at downtown malls and other "silver bullet" big-ticket items that failed, canned experiences pushed through by developers with backing from the tourism industry, when a fraction of those dollars devoted to restoring the town's authentic infrastructure, or promoting farmers markets and other low-cost community events, would create the distinctive, pedestrian-friendly atmosphere high-value visitors and employers seek. Better, not bigger.

MacKaye reminded us that every place *has* a unique identity, although he was concerned as early as the 1950s that Americans were doing their best to undermine the distinctive character of many towns—wiping away the diversity Jane Jacobs revered, fabricating Kunstler's geography of nowhere, surrendering to a car-oriented "asphalt nation" that values passage more than place, says Jane Holtz Kay. Successful place-making is often just a matter of getting out of the way, MacKaye believed, and allowing a community's authentic self to emerge naturally: "The job is not to 'plan' but to *reveal*," he said to fellow urban planners, encouraging an *organic* approach to place-making that hinges on words some planners habitually erase from their dictionary: *submission* and *restraint*. "Only in the act of submission," Wallace Stegner writes, "is the sense of place realized and a sustainable relationship between people and earth established."

Sounds swell, but it's all too muddled. What the heck does it mean? It's mountain thinking: Allow what's already there to improve and help it along within the margins of your history and heritage—blend in naturally and culturally, urged architect Frank Lloyd Wright and planner Frederick Law Olmstead. Allow place to reveal itself by adapting the needs and identities of people to those of streets, the health and history of mountains to those of buildings, the values of citizens to those of landscapes. Rybczynski writes, "this is the city considered as a kind or organism: cohesive, balanced, indivisible. Medieval towns are organic—their layouts look natural rather than manmade." It's fitting into and respecting the history and "values in the soil," rather than the growth machine's inversion of that practice, as Willa Cather's quotation at the beginning of this conversation illustrates: "accommodating themselves to the scene in which they found themselves." Translate the organic code to tourism planning, and it's the difference between "development," done in concert with a community's natural and cultural heritage, which of course you have to know, and blunt "growth," whose calculus often has little concern for heritage. Towns will change and evolve, no doubt about it; it's not if but how, to which Tony Hiss advises: "Make sure that when we change a place the change is agreed upon and nurtures our growth as capable and responsible people while also protecting the natural environment and developing jobs and homes enough for all." Recognizing that humans *will* use and alter their environment, that much of what we call home is contrived, others have characterized the organic approach as the "garden ethic," noting that our place in and dependence on nature, if nurtured like a family garden, does not necessarily mean that our impact "will always be negative," writes Michael Pollan. So is your symbol of touristic change a healthy garden and an inviting streetscape, or a charred stump and strip mall? *This* is your most valuable place-based tourism asset, not only institutions and purpose-built attractions.

Organic tourism development is the difference between tearing down an old gas station to throw up another bland Taco Bell, and working with the community to turn it into a restaurant or playground, assets for residents that also lend character to the street. It's the difference between converting an old home into an elegant B&B and demolishing it for a boxy Motel 6. It's the difference between scraping a hillside for another Big Mart, and partnering with land trusts to buy and preserve the open space as a cultural legacy *and* tourism asset. It's the difference between allowing a stream to meander through town on its own terms and the Army Corp of Engineers de-meandering it, so as to "improve upon nature." The organic approach not only enhances community character, it's often more cost-effective, and not only because of lower infrastructure outlays. Daily and Ellison tell us, for example, that when Napa, California, returned a managed, cemented river to its natural course, business boomed, real estate appreciated, and visitors returned. To plan organically, then, create a "place matrix" of sorts and apply its standards and indicators to every one of your conversations:

- **Diversity:** a vigorous mix of design, scale, and function.
- **Balance:** vitality and harmony, physically and aesthetically.
- **Connectivity:** accord among resources as well as pleasurable passage between them.
- **Association:** local appreciation, regional consideration.
- **Differentiation:** a story that distinguishes your community.
- **Adaptability:** long-term vision that accounts for change.
- **Appropriateness:** within the margins of your natural and cultural heritage.
- **Yield:** sustainable economic networks that circulate profits locally.
- **and Mountain Thinking:** Is this what the mountain would do?

Sure, these concepts are as vague as "beauty" and you'll argue endlessly over what they mean and how they apply, but consider the alternative view, which is anything *but* vague. Are you factory farming and growing the same plastic peaches people can find anywhere, asks Masumoto, or sowing and reaping an organic place—a "microbrewed community" instead of another can of Bud? Are you contributing to the health of the "mountain," which then returns sustenance to the community, or working against it? The good news is there are countless architects, planners, urbanists, and scholars who do this work, who *can* quantify and design according to the standards in your matrix; who *are* applying the principles of mountain thinking to community development; who *do* understand and build upon the relationship between environments and economics. Your task is to engage and encourage their vision, using tourism planning as the tool to unlock the conversation. The process might not lead to "more" tourists but, as is the case with organic fruit, the product is so much sweeter, you build bonds with your clientele through story, and the practice leaves valuable nutrients in the soil.

### *"Decide": Can We? Should We?*

One of the handful of helpful planning practices your community might conduct is a design charrette using modern imaging software that allows citizens to actually see how, as Pope says, the "Parts answering parts will slide into a whole." How do buildings fit with one another? Trees with streets? Sidewalks with traffic? Hillsides with houses? Ideally, the view should feel as if the pieces belong there, like a stream snaking through a pasture, discovering a route and pace conditioned by its place. Architectural charrettes and related visioning forums illustrate that "place" is not a question of how many parts, a functionalist view that simply adds up the pieces, but a matter of relationships. Pattern trumps volume.

Important as they are, though, these planning exercises are only one phase, because place is, if nothing else, a "story happening many times," according to a Kwakiutl saying. In the classic *Poetics of Space*, Gaston Bachelard agrees, pointing out that "sense of place" goes beyond the physicality of space and aesthetics of design. Home, he says, is more than a dimensioned, walled dwelling: "it is also an embodiment of dreams." Buildings, streets, and mountains hold our dreams and shared narratives; the way we care for them reflects who we are—providing context, mirroring values, capturing emotions. *Story.* Tourism historian Maxine Feifer talks about the pleasure "of *reading* Paris" and other landscapes. And when read together as chapters of the same book, the built, natural, and social stories shed light on one another, illuminate patterns, and round out the narrative, say urbanists Beatley and Manning: "The evolution of our built environment, and the ways in which we modify and interact with the natural environment, are themselves a manifestation of our society values." *Story.* Most visitors don't analytically dissect locations, however, and so the challenge is to provide guests an *experience* of how the parts fit together, including their place in the story: "He cried the relief he felt at finally seeing the pattern, the way all the stories fit together—the old stories, the war stories, their stories—to become the story that was still being told" (Leslie Marmon Silko, *Ceremony*).

From an operational point of view, an integrated approach to place-making, one that incorporates ecological and organic applications, requires getting out of our silos—not only the tourism and place silos, but also the silos within silos. For instance, the NGOs and other groups engaged in environmental, cultural, and preservation activities all dabble in the same business—the story of a place. Organizations promoting ecotourism and heritage tourism often appeal to the same "experiential" visitor, but all culture takes place *within* a natural setting, and culture and character will always be "shaped by the landscape," says Terry Tempest Williams, just as we shape *it*. Williams reveals in *Refuge*, a personal narrative that captures the indispensable link between people, place, and story, that nature isn't empty land, there are stories in the earth: "As a people and as a family, we have a sense of history. And our history is tied to land." When one of my state's early "tourists," John Wesley Powell, returned from his 1869 expedition down the Colorado River, his report didn't focus solely on the Grand Canyon's amazing geology, but surveyed as well the languages and customs of indigenous peoples. It's not just pretty rocks and a river—people lived there! *That* was the experience of this magnificent landscape for Powell, made so much richer by the interactions between land and people. We can think of our communities the same way, writes historian William Cronon in *Uncommon Ground*, because history can seldom be truly appreciated unless we realize how much of the story involves interactions between people and nature.

Consequently, when you develop museum exhibitions, interpretive ramadas, nature park signage, walking tour pamphlets, and basic hospitality fulfillment materials, ask: What role did nature play in shaping our past and determining the present? What does our streetscape reveal about the community's history and values? How does the natural setting influence arts and crafts? How do our political and social expressions affect downtown design? How does it all fit as one ecosystem, one mountain? As the art critic and social observer Lucy Lippard notes, place "is about connections, what surrounds it, what formed it, what happened there, what will happen there." *This* is where the story of a place gets interesting; *this* is where you differentiate your community from the one down the road and build narrative bonds with guests. And the cool thing is, give the experience away to visitors and you still get to keep it for yourself. Win-win.

Designing a tourism program around a compelling, multifaceted story, with community actors moving forward together as one, is a sensible and feasible approach for almost any place, regardless of size. Sadly, though, I can't count how many towns I've visited where the historical society and art museum seldom cooperate, where the zoo and land trust don't even like one another, where the

APPLICATION 4.1

historic preservation guild and parks department have never met. *Fragmented* is the operative word. Whether it's personalities or power or politics, this schisming of place is ultimately short-sighted, says Priscilla Boniface: "we can no longer afford to 'walk alone.' We must act in concert, adopting an integrated approach." Beyond the fact that a fragmented design doesn't invite visitors into the full story, the nonprofit groups and public agencies charged with overseeing the various forms of alternative tourism often don't have the necessary resources or clout to be as effectual individually as they might collectively.

Tourism officials often note, for example, that few heritage attractions are "destination drivers" themselves, and so a typical response is to design itineraries, connecting regional museums and other heritage sites. While a step in the right direction, itineraries generally overlook product development and they are often little more than marketing ploys that perpetuate the functionalist, more-is-better ethic: a *multi*dimensional approach that simply adds up the parts as opposed to an *inter*dimensional scheme that explains how the parts relate to one another (ecological) and the broader community narrative (organic). Absent a shared interpretive approach, the hospitality juggernaut can wash over the small scattered "projects," no matter how nicely linked in brochures and websites, and, with no collective eyes on the ball, the further misapplication of place for tourism is probable, as recent history suggests.

It was only in 1983, for instance, that "ecotourism" was coined as a discipline (of course the practice existed long before), and tracing that short history, as Martha Honey does in *Ecotourism and Sustainable Development*, one finds the early expressions are unambiguous about purpose: to preserve nature, regional traditions, and local economies. Profit is a tool for preservation and should never be the tail that wags the dog. Today countless tourism programs use "green" or "eco" language, appealing to society's growing interest in and support for safeguarding and experiencing nature (granted, a mixed message). But the reality does not always live up to the advertisers' lingo, and in myopic pursuit of more revenue "ecotourism" attractions can damage the environment, water down local customs, and squeeze out small business—a practice opponents termed "greenwashing" in the early 1990s (a harsher critic would just call it lying). The word has slipped into everyday dialect to indicate the pimping of any healthy label, such as advertising peaches as "organic" when they don't meet the standards; using pictures of Bambi and other adorable forest creatures to advertise a paper company's commitment to recycling, at the same time it lobbies against clear-cutting restrictions; or marketing a new residential village as "green" when it's the typical suburb with a few "heritage trails," brick sidewalks, park benches, and old-fashioned street lights plopped down—the "history kit" approach. Concept, not culture. Who's minding the store?

Similarly, the misrepresentation of social or cultural assets to attract vacationers, such as romanticizing or mythologizing a local event, person, or custom, has recently been termed "bluewashing." Consider Tombstone's salute to the Earp boys' sixty-second shootout at the OK Corral, every hour on the hour, or the stereotypical and occasionally inaccurate ways American Indian or Amish cultures are used to hock doohickeys or brand entire regions, sometimes without the inclusion of or approval from the exploited societies—a practice that borders on "human zoos." Beyond the cultural and environmental ethics of bluewashing and greenwashing, which dilute or even destroy authentic customs and lands, such practices can alienate residents who are proud of their heritage, warts and all; and, from a financial point of view, cartoon replicas of local traditions increasingly appeal to drive-by tourists—the two-hour, ten-dollar visitors around whom it's difficult to build an equitable and sustainable hospitality economy. Again, who is the industry responsible to?

Although place-making might be a dicey and often contested terrain fraught with more than a few interpretive and perhaps political landmines, a vigorous conceptual investment in the story is necessary if communities are to avoid the misapplications of place, as well as benefit from the possibilities, of which there are many. It's rare to visit a town absent a possibility with which to begin—a neighborhood, trail system, arts district, regional cuisine, good museum—and if you ask why one place succeeds while another with similar resources languishes, it's often because a core group of people acted on that possibility. Regardless of what Gertrude Stein said about "no there there," every place *has* the potential of "place," every town *is* a story, and through conversations with the entire community, not just historians and the museum crew, you're likely to uncover that narrative and determine if and how it can be shared with guests. However, as entertaining and necessary as theoretical discussions about the nature of place might be for some, eventually you have to ask: How do we pay for the dang thing?

## *"Find Resources": Tenacious Be*

Your local tourism bureau is probably a marketing agency supported in part by bed taxes, a line item in the city's general fund, and perhaps membership fees—or a combination of all three. The same holds for state-level tourism programs, where the typical agency is a multimillion-dollar firm devoted primarily to marketing your commonwealth worldwide. Certainly there are different versions: some well-financed, others neglected; some fully state agencies, others more privately held; some that focus on international sales, others preferring to concentrate locally; some that are public relations firms and that's all, a few that dabble in capacity building and product development. In general, though, the mission of most local and statewide "tourism" organizations is to attract more people to the region, and that's what their budgets support. I certainly don't begrudge these organizations their advertising dollars, and many should have more.

It's welcome news that some state tourism budgets, like California's, have increased significantly in the past few years alone: millions of dollars available to research the spending and staying habits of tourists, provide supplemental support to local agencies, and investigate the best and most cost-effective promotional strategies: the web? travel magazines? fulfillment packages? partnerships? television ads? Bottom line: there's a lot of time, money, and smarts that go into developing promotional campaigns, but where is the equivalent investment in the products, the very things the advertisers sell? Tourism today is far too important and influential to be thought of as a marketing responsibility only.

There *is* one sector of the industry that does a great deal of R&D for product development—the private sector. Corporations building hotels, golf courses, shopping malls, casinos, theme parks, and similar doodads conduct significant research and line up well-heeled investors, *and* they are sometimes eligible for tax breaks and other public "incentives." Distinguished by a for-profit motive, these niches are among the most influential voices around the table at local and state strategy sessions, and, through their lobbying associations, with elected officials. For place-based tourism, on the other hand, product development tends to be the responsibility of nonprofit organizations such as history museums and environmental groups, public agencies like your city's historic preservation or recreation department, or the grossly underfunded federal park and land-management agencies. These groups usually occupy at best token seats around many tourism planning tables, even though history or nature may be the area's main attraction, and their relations with politicians are often more sociable than effective. Consequently, funding schemes that support place-based product development are typically distinguished by the following:

- **Lack of Funds:** It goes without saying that few of these programs have enough staff or funding to fulfill *their* missions, let alone provide sufficient resources for additional community projects. Arts, history, parks, humanities, and preservation budgets are often considered "frills," their funding generally remains level at best from decade to decade, and their appropriations are almost always under attack from certain quarters. The wonderful exceptions should be the norm.

- **Silo Funding:** Product development funding, such as it is, is scattered across local, state, and federal agencies, as well as foundations and corporations, whose policies tend to exacerbate "silo thinking," rather than an integrated interpretation of place. You might be able to raise money for an arts project, but try to weave historic preservation into the application. That's another agency or grant category.

- **Tourism Nada:** Product funding usually has no direct connection to tourism. In fact, when applying to some agencies don't even mention your community wants to preserve a historic building, for example, to support the local hospitality agenda. Purists who view tourism as a crude commercial exploitation of the historic site might score your application lower.

- **Rural Challenges:** What private funding exists from foundations and corporations, especially six-figure gifts, typically serves large metropolitan institutions, rarely finding its way to a rural arts group, preservation society, or history museum. Likewise, if you operate a modest cultural center in a small town, the chances of securing a large federal grant—or even being able to complete the paperwork—are slim.

- **Projects! Projects!** Most awards are intended for projects, not staff, capacity building, maintenance, or other necessary day-to-day operations. Civic tourism is about a community moving forward together—its built, cultural, and natural actors—with a new region-wide vision for place-based development. It's about the necessary infrastructure, not simply another heritage trail or museum exhibit, as welcome as they might be.

- **Not Dependable:** Regardless of source, almost all product funding is episodic, coming and going at the whim of city councils, legislatures, Congress, and foundation boards of directors. Most support is generally tied to grants, which can never be depended on from one year to the next.

Missing here is a long-term, concerted, tourism-centric effort, similar to the approach to marketing, that helps communities build capacity to play the tourism game, offers assistance to support citizen inquiries into the relationship between place and tourism, and, significantly, provides funds to improve and maintain existing products as well as develop new ones.

Local and state tourism agencies can make any museum look good in a website or fancy promotional magazine, but what happens when visitors show up on Saturday and there's a sign pinned to the door that says, "Hours: Tues. & Thurs. 1–4 PM"? Are they likely to return? Or I've stumbled upon several versions of this note: "If you'd like to see the museum, go to the 7-11 and ask for Marge. She has the key." Other times the site is open, but it's staffed with volunteers—well-meaning people whose commitment you treasure, but who often have no museum experience, and the place feels like grandma's attic: a buffalo head here, an old sewing machine there (circa 1883, the label says), a painting of somebody I don't know. I drop a few dollars in the donation box on the way out, but I have no sense of what this community's story is or why people are proud to call it home. And still we hear that "cultural heritage" is a tourism priority. I leave the museum and drive to a trailhead I used to know, but a gated community that creeps halfway up the hillside blocks access to the mountain. And still we hear that "nature" is a tourism priority. I drive out of town through miles of placelessness, "a low-grade uniform environment," forecast Lewis Mumford in the 1960s, "from which escape is impossible," a clutter of commercial crap unhealthy to the eyes, lungs, and pocketbook. And still we hear that "sense of place" is a tourism priority.

APPLICATION 4.3

If your city and state can appropriate tens of millions of dollars for tourism promotion, why isn't there an equivalent program that invests in "sense of place" for tourism development, which is both an economic and quality of life asset? It's sadly ironic, for example, that development stunts ramrodded through city councils and legislatures by the growth industry allow towns to apply for public funds to build golf courses and theme parks, but not to improve their local museum for tourism. I'm not suggesting we simply throw money at cultural institutions so they can create new projects. Place-based tourism funding programs should:

- **Mandate Partnerships:** Collaboration between the heritage community, tourism industry, government agencies, and citizen associations should be factored into all programs, so the community moves forward together with one voice, one agenda—so the entire community is thought of as a heritage destination, not just the museum. In other words, funding programs should be designed to encourage "place committees" and similar inclusive, citizen-driven units. Support activities should further ecological thinking, so tourism is positioned as an essential component of community planning.

- **Build Capacity:** Funding mechanisms should build in ample planning up front, so communities are prepared to act responsibly and productively. Programs could require local teams to complete capacity-building training before the community is eligible to apply for implementation support. Many of the conceptual challenges outlined here, i.e., involving the public, interpreting the story, and uncovering place, should be reviewed in the training sessions.

- **Sustain Success.** Assistance programs should be designed to meet the *specific* needs of communities, not to enforce a standardized format for place-making, and they should cover multiyear cycles so as to avoid the funding spasms that typically occur. The financial support might not be sufficient, but most towns can depend on a certain level of local and state funding for tourism marketing. The same should be true for product development.

- **Measure Results:** Programs should mandate and provide funds to complete outcome measurements, in order to evaluate economic, environmental, and social results—that is, a triple-bottom-line report. Funding agencies should require that interim and final reports are shared in public meetings.

There's simply no excuse for allocating dollars to advertising and pennies to product, and there are even fewer excuses for tourism officials to stonewall appropriations for place-based product development, when these funding programs, such as the pioneering efforts in Connecticut and Iowa, provide travel bureaus better attractions to market. Often marketing agencies see a finite pie, where every dollar allocated to product is a dollar not available for promotion. Some cities and counties, for example, are experimenting with setting aside a portion of bed taxes for parks and museums, a move unfortunately blocked by some business interests, which is short-sighted, ineffectual, and self-defeating. The focus should be on expanding the pie, not scrapping over a few slices, and investing in product helps grow that pie in two ways: First, the hospitality industry's goodwill helps keep the place sector and general public in its corner, organizations and people who can assist with advocacy and product development. Also, numerous surveys indicate that a quality heritage product prompts visitors to stay longer (typically a half-day), return, and tell others about the experience. Those extra stays and visits, from guests known to spend more, supplement bed taxes and other tourism revenues, a percentage of which eventually ends up in marketing programs.

Thankfully, states, counties, and cities are beginning to recognize the logic of investing in the story—the very products and experiences that provide a sense of belonging for tourists, not to mention community assets for residents. These resource programs look different in different places—some managed by a tourism agency, others conducted by an arts or humanities council, several headquartered in parks, historical societies, and government economic development sectors. No doubt your citizen committee will encounter political and turf battles, as well as philosophical disputes, when you attempt to establish a similar investment strategy, whether local or statewide, but the reality is you probably *can* do this. Study the advocacy schemes and funding structures of places where it is working, several of which are described in the Applications; marshal economic development and quality of life arguments, either from this essay, the referenced publications, or websites such as Cultural Heritage Tourism; identify champions on your city council and in your legislature, by appealing to both the economic and place-enhancing benefits of a responsible tourism ethic; build grassroots support among the business community, the media, cultural sectors, hospitality allies, and residents by framing the conversation as a public good and a public responsibility; and, through museum associations and other networks, reach across city and county boundaries to other communities engaged in the same work to build regional and statewide affiliations that can carry the message. And be tenacious.

### Possibility Unbound: Promising Ampersands

Back to core values: If your local travel sector genuinely endorses and incorporates healthy place-based development models, such as the New Economy, it can enhance, empower, and pull together the historic, natural, social, and cultural ingredients that make place *place*—rendering the parts more dynamic and effective collectively than any are individually. Emboldening place in this manner benefits a community's tourism operation in two huge ways (imagine your town here):

First, a vibrant sense of place is among the most compelling, profitable, and sustainable tourism products, attracting high-value visitors and allowing your

APPLICATION 3.3

town to retain and enhance its character as it jumpstarts its economy. Numerous local, statewide, and national studies confirm the favorable economic impact of alternative tourism. Granted, you'll hear from some travel and economic development officials that culture and heritage are boring: "People don't really travel for that. We need an outlet mall or water park." Although evidence suggests otherwise, I've heard the same from some economic planning quarters, and it took me a long time to realize that *they* think it's boring and *they* don't visit cultural sites, mountain trails, art galleries, or historic districts when they travel, which is to say they're out of step with the growing numbers who do—the growing *profitable* numbers who do. So who do you want designing your local tourism campaign: people who care about the town's historic character and natural resources, or those who, when they travel, only visit malls and are convinced that's what everyone else wants?

Second, your local tourism actors should consider the political points to be scored, because the current plan just ain't workin'! Consider that the United States is one of the few nations in the Western world without a cabinet-level tourism post. As I write, the US Department of Commerce has budgeted less than $4 million for travel promotion, while Malaysia will spend nearly $118 million and Turkey $80 million. The figures are equally sorry at some state and local levels, but you probably already know that. If we are to turn residents and elected officials into effective industry advocates, a new approach is necessary, one that begins by rethinking tourism's role in our communities. Simply, the hackneyed economic development drumbeat has rendered many potential supporters deaf. When hidden costs are factored in and phony multiplier gimmicks factored out, some people just don't believe the numbers, while others would gladly forgo the financial incentives if they could "just have my old town back."

The ingredients of place discussed here, on the other hand—cultures, neighborhoods, landscapes—are critical to the *quality* development advanced by the various voices campaigning for the New Economy, all dancing atop Aldo Leopold's mountain. In practicing tourism as a means to help citizens embrace, understand, and reveal a place's distinctive cultural fabric, the industry comes to be seen and valued by residents, businesses, and elected officials as a tool for leveraging the healthiest kind of community development, and a new awareness and respect develops: The New Economy can emerge and prosper through tourism, if allowed, as can civil society and a healthy ecology of place. Oars up.

In the end, the "poetry and politics of place" represent two sides of the same industry coin, an industry wedded to place like no other; and in that sense tourism can be *the* tool, to paraphrase Stegner, that helps communities create a society that is the equal to their scenery. To do so, industry leaders and community caretakers must come together and link contemporary development policies—creative economics, civic engagement, and place-based investment—to an industry that can benefit from and contribute to their integration like few others. Design your community conversations around product & process, poetry & politics, scenery & society—with tourism as the ampersand.

# *"Invest in the Story": Conversation Starters*

1. **Place Making:** What institutions in your region focus on the preservation and improvement of cultural, natural, and social ingredients of place? How well-funded are they? What is your community's history of supporting cultural projects, environmental causes, education? Is there a concentrated focus on place-making, or does it tend to be scattered and episodic? Might there be a way to reorganize training and funding under one agency?

2. **Place Finding:** If people and organizations in your community talk about "sense of place," are they primarily referring to a built notion, a natural one, or a historic sense of place? Or perhaps a combination? Do the agencies that represent these different characteristics of place have a history of working together? If so, where does that collaboration show up? If not, why? Do residents complain about the "loss of place" or the "loss of community" and, if so, do they ever blame the tourism sector? Can you identify local tourism products that represent "greenwashing" or "bluewashing"?

3. **Place Funding:** Have there been recent attempts in your community to develop a capacity-building and funding scheme to assist museums, Main Street programs, archaeological sites, and other heritage institutions, beyond the usual funding programs at the state or federal levels? If so, what has been the reception? How might you restructure tourism funding so more visitors' dollars are reinvested in place-based products? If you attempt to create a product development funding mechanism, will traditional tourism voices support or block your efforts? Do you know political allies who might help start this conversation?

4. **Book Discussion Idea:** *The Death and Life of Great American Cities*, by Jane Jacobs (1961). In the early 1960s, a resident from Greenwich Village took on the city's powerful transportation lobby, which wanted to ram a freeway through her neighborhood. Jane Jacobs's research and activism eventually turned into one of the most famous books in urban planning, and her arguments are often couched in place-making terms that still resonate today.

# MOUNTAIN REDUX
## *Learn the Flowers*

*I half-closed my eyes and imagined this was the spot*
*where everything I'd ever lost since my childhood*
*had washed up. . . .*
~ Kazuo Ishiguro, *Never Let Me Go*

The wispy voice of Nick Drake on "Saturday's Sun" accompanies my drive east on a lonesome patch of highway, the sun setting in the rearview mirror, a yellow moon hanging low and large on the horizon ahead. It's a mild spring dusk, and the rental car's windows are down as I return to a small Montana town I visited eighteen months ago. Drake's ruminating about "people and places I have known" could be the soundtrack for some of these meetings, where we talk in ampersands about how "people and places" might come together to serve local economies and cultures. I've come to believe the hillsides folding in on me along this drive have known all along.

Nature is nothing if not elegant, adaptable, and utilitarian. Shaking our nineteenth-century Western belief system to its core, the reluctant Mr. Darwin told us that, after billions of years practicing, nature had figured it out. To appreciate its magnificence, recall that we marshaled all of our science and technology to duplicate nature for only two years in Biosphere II. That the imitation model broke was not a failure, for it showed how incredible the authentic process is, and it reminded us that humans cannot stand apart from and manipulate nature like a machine, as if we're godlike puppeteers. "The 'control of nature' is a phrase conceived in arrogance," warns Rachel Carson in the last paragraph of *Silent Spring*. Ultimately our tools only make more tools, and they tend to muck up the works. Find another way. More and more "another way" is there *in* nature, staring us in the face. Learning from nature's instincts, which Aldo Leopold termed "thinking like a mountain" and entrepreneurs today call "biomimicry," is influencing economics, medicine, architecture, agriculture, manufacturing, and energy. Why not community development? Why not tourism? Especially since one of tourism's main products *is* nature.

Passing by a wood-and-granite welcome sign and entering the west end of town, I note trees that weren't there before, a narrower streetscape, and a fair number of pedestrians. On one corner a man plays guitar, his case open on the sidewalk for donations, a handful of people listening. Muffled talk and occasional laughter spills out from the open doors of shops and restaurants, while indigo mountains loom in the near distance—a backdrop to a friendly variety of late nineteenth-century facades, and I think of Jane Jacobs, who passed away this week: "an intricate and close-grained diversity of uses that give each other constant mutual support." There's mutuality here, someone cares, the place works.

I check into the hotel my hosts have arranged, a wonderful dun-colored 1890 structure built with mining money and refurbished to its original luster. At the front desk, I ask where the nearest history museum is. That's something I often do, to get a sense of whether the hospitality and cultural sectors are aware of one another. The young clerk not only tells me where the facility is, she also says the exhibition about Lewis and Clark is "pretty decent." The museum, I'm told, began hosting receptions for travel industry employees last year. It also provides free admission for hospitality workers and their families, and hosts an awards program that recognizes businesses that support the town's historic preservation activities. Her boss is on the museum board. Cool.

"Are you here for the tourism thing?" she asks. I tell her, yes, I'm the tourism guy and I'll be speaking tomorrow. Then she asks the question I dread getting on a twenty-second elevator ride: "What is this civic tourism?" When I need the Cliff Notes version, as I do now standing before this smiling twenty-something, I generally say it's an "extension" of ecotourism, heritage tourism, and other alternative forms that have proliferated over the past three decades. That may mean little, which I imagine is the case with Heather from Oregon, a brushed-copper nametag says. Most people know of ecotourism, and many have heard of cultural or heritage tourism, but what it means to "extend" them generally doesn't compute. Truth is, I'm still figuring it out, but I've only come so far as to figure out that figuring it out means not trying to figure it out. Zen tourism.

"I majored in hospitality at Arizona State," she smiles, "and I wrote my master's thesis on ecotourism around Sedona." I've misjudged Heather, who tells me she's just moved to town and eventually wants to work in a national park. For another ten minutes we talk in the hushed, historic lobby amid shadows and quiet pastels about her concern that ecotourism and other place-based models tend to be "elitist," as are the "trendy towns" I advocate—a familiar barb. "Civic tourism does not lean toward creating more of David Brooks's BOBO villages," I say, "and in truth we're more aligned with social justice movements than the trendy Restoration Hardware sect." In fact, I don't doubt that towns will continue to build big box stores and sprawling suburbs, which some people *do* want. The problem comes when that's the *only* form of development, wiping away diversity, choice, and sense of place. And let's be honest, the boxes and sprawl will get built anyway; they don't need our backing, but those speaking for quality development do.

"It's just that most of the great towns are not affordable," Heather complains. One reason they are more expensive, of course, is that there are so few of them. "It's like organic fruit," I say, "economies of scale, so let's build more wonderful communities." A problem with my argument is that, just as with farming, government subsidies and other policies tend to encourage drab town planning, making it less complicated and more profitable to build characterless "generica," as Kunstler calls it, just as agribusiness is incentivized to grow plastic peaches on factory farms. Oddly, our policies make it more difficult and more expensive to grow fruit and towns in ways that restore the land, save resources, and deliver a healthier product. The reverse is clearly preferable, and tourism should put its shoulder to that political wheel. "*Everyone*," I say a little too loudly, "not just the wealthy, deserves 'great good places,' people shouldn't have to settle for less, and tourism can help communities sow and harvest those places. Sure, you want to create a community that's attractive to high-value visitors, the 'elites,' if you will, but it's like NPR or PBS: your major donors make the product available to everyone."

Heather says she'll think about it and come to the community meeting tomorrow. I leave her my card and ride up to the third floor in an elevator made to fit one of the small cages that used to require an operator. It's not much more than four-by-four, and luckily, with my luggage, there isn't more than one of me. I take the key—no plastic credit card gizmo here—and open room 36, full of hope.

To climb these coming crests
one word to you, to
you and your children:

*stay together*
*learn the flowers*
*go light*

~Gary Snyder, "For the Children"

Hope resides foremost in people, and if my experiences are an indication, there's reason to be hopeful. As I talk with citizens across the country about how tourism does or doesn't work in their communities, I sense agreement from many quarters: economic development agencies, cultural groups, environmentalists, urban planners, the public, even tourism bureaus. Many people love their communities and know they have a viable tourism "product," but they are concerned, on one hand, that unrestrained growth, sometimes supported by the hospitality industry, will eventually tart up the town and bury its unique heritage, or, on the other hand, that tourism has never become the financial windfall boosters promised, providing little more than minimum-wage jobs and tacky attractions that seldom benefit residents, many who see little value in the current design. At one forum the town's vice-mayor said his residents would vote "overwhelmingly" to ban tourists if the question were put to a vote. He's not alone. Among many citizens, there's a collective understanding of and agreement about the issues and, I sense, a renewed energy to try something different once presented with, as Rosamund Zander titles it, "the art of possibility."

Another grounds for hope can be found in education, specifically the colleges and universities that teach hospitality, such as the program from which Heather graduated. Like the practice of tourism itself, teaching tourism is a recent and still evolving enterprise. The earliest university programs typically slotted travel into "recreation," "community planning," or a related business discipline, and students were exposed to little more than how to market an attraction, develop a hotel organizational chart, complete a spreadsheet, and other "trades" of tourism. Today, when I meet with hospitality students, many are aware of the industry's social and environmental obligations, and some are familiar with restorative economic theory, such as the triple-bottom-line approach or the writings of Paul Hawken, E. O. Wilson, and other thinkers with something to say on the matter. Even conventional textbooks, such as Goeldner and Ritchie's *Tourism: Principles, Practices, Philosophies*, now in its umpteenth edition, broach issues of cultural sensitivity, economic inequity, and environmental abuse. Among today's students there's an acceptance that tourism is something more than "heads in beds" and Internet marketing: most are fluent in the vocabularies of alternative tourism, they're more socially and environmentally conscious than students a decade ago, and they appreciate the argument that tourism officials must act as responsible corporate citizens—that tourism is *not* a "boutique industry" off in the corner by itself, but rather an important part of a social ecology. Tourism studies today often confirm that principle by reaching across disciplines, from agriculture to law, economics to history—even sustainability studies. Happily, the next generation of hoteliers, chamber of commerce officials, and city managers will take for granted and work to implement much of what we've been discussing.

Hope also can be found among the many cultural advocates, environmentalists, city planners, economists, and tourism officials who are already working together, serving as models for those of us who still wonder if place-based tourism can live up to its promises. From heritage tours in Harlem to heritage trails in Arizona, we find evidence that the "culture of tourism" and the "tourism of culture" can indeed foster pride in place *and* build sustainable economies. The finest of these programs are designed and conducted by people who cherish their communities and neighborhoods, and many will tell you that a personal connection to place—in ways that go beyond a purely commercial transaction—makes their investment better than worthwhile. After two decades of working with community caretakers, I realize that they often live where they do because of the sense of belonging that provides satisfying social harbor. The loudest voices of the growth machine often say that it's jobs that make a place attractive. Get the other stuff right and jobs, good jobs, will follow; but privilege only the growth mantra in a dead-end quest for "more," and you risk alienating residents, undermining the health of the community they love, and putting a big dent in the possibility of tourism. Employment is one element in the ecosystem, an important one to be sure, but if we have a say in the decision, we stay where we are—we "stay put," counsels Scott Sanders—and we commit to our place, because we grow to appreciate the cultural, natural, and social networks that surround, serve, and bond us.

Tomorrow I fly home to Arizona to meet a friend from back East and play tour guide, showing off our grand vistas—mountains, deserts, towns, and cultures. Certainly we'll visit the Grand Canyon, Monument Valley, and Flagstaff, northern locations never to be missed. But like your state, it's more than a few destination drivers that make me feel as if I belong in and to this place. It's the world's largest stand of Ponderosa pines near Prescott; the glowing purple dusk behind Texas Canyon and Chiricahua territory; the jaw-dropping awe at Hopi; river cultures near Yuma and border cultures in and through Nogales; the unrivaled splendor of the White Mountains and the stunning clarity and serenity of deserts; and urban experiences, from Jerome's small-town funkiness to Scottsdale's museums and Tucson's barrio revivals. And the people who care for them. We can and should take pride in the majesty of our place, but machines loom on the horizon and there is work to be done. A mountain is thinking and tourism nears, ready for the climb. Or not.

> The song of the waters is audible to every ear, but there is other music in these hills, by no means audible to all. To hear even a few notes of it you must first live here for a long time, and you must know the speech of hills and rivers. Then on a still night, when the campfire is low and the Pleiades have climbed over rimrocks, sit quietly and listen for a wolf to howl, and think hard of everything you have seen and tried to understand. Then you may hear it—a vast pulsing harmony—its score inscribed on a thousand hills, its notes the lives and deaths of plants and animals, its rhythms spanning the seconds and the centuries.
>
> —Aldo Leopold, "Song of the Gavilan"

# APPLICATIONS

*Knowing is not enough; we must apply.*
*Willing is not enough; we must do.* ~Goethe

The following exercises, suggestions, and practices are offered as ways into the central themes of the preceding four conversations. Additional applications, as well as extended and updated versions of these examples, can be found at the civic tourism website: www.civictourism.org.

# Place-based Tourism

*Cultural tourism can survive only if its asset base is managed in a sustainable manner and sustainability can be achieved only if tourism and cultural heritage management work in partnership.* ~Bob McKercher and Hilary du Cros, *Cultural Tourism: The Partnership Between Tourism and Cultural Heritage Management*

One topic sidestepped here is the definition discussion—the differences between "cultural tourism" and "cultural heritage tourism," for example. I also steer clear of the debates about "culture," "history," and "nostalgia," and I leave to others the disputes over what constitutes a "tourist" or "visitor," as well as the parsing of tourism typologies ("explorer," "recreational"). Those discussions have been batted around in countless studies, and while definitions often matter politically the wordsmithing can bore the public, and the linguistic nitpicking can result in a missing-the-forest-for-the-trees conversation. Instead, this essay uses "place-based" and other integrated terms, which might encompass:

• Adventure Tourism • Agritourism • Community Tourism • Cultural Heritage Tourism • Cultural Tourism • Dark Tourism • Ecotourism • Geotourism • Heritage Tourism • Life-Seeing Tourism • Literary Tourism • Social Justice Tourism • Sustainable Tourism • Urban Tourism • Volunteer Tourism

And so on. In addition, these schools may splinter into more branches, such as ecotourism providing a home for "adventure tourism" and "nature tourism." Regardless, most represent an approach to travel designed around at least one of three *experiences* of place: natural, cultural, or built. For most communities, "sense of place" exists in the sweet spot where the three intersect, shed light on one another, and create a "story." Consequently, the language here leans toward the comprehensive "place" or "experiential" expressions instead of specific models. Additionally, civic tourism is less concerned about definitions than the *process* behind the approach—that is, making it work.

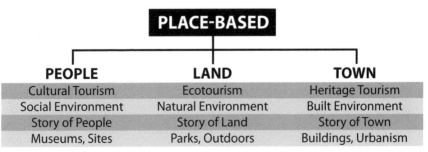

| PLACE-BASED | | |
|---|---|---|
| **PEOPLE** | **LAND** | **TOWN** |
| Cultural Tourism | Ecotourism | Heritage Tourism |
| Social Environment | Natural Environment | Built Environment |
| Story of People | Story of Land | Story of Town |
| Museums, Sites | Parks, Outdoors | Buildings, Urbanism |

## "FRAME FLIPPING": APPLICATION 1.1
# 4 To Do: Web, Read, Learn, Try

1. **Web:** *Cultural Heritage Tourism.* If you're not a frequenter of this website, bookmark it and visit regularly. Managed in part by the National Trust for Historic Preservation, the site provides a snapshot of place-based tourism programs around the country, manuals and other advice for getting started, and, importantly, economic impact studies you can adapt for advocacy work.

2. **Read:** *Issues in Cultural Tourism Studies*, by Melanie K. Smith. Several recent books provide a solid introduction to place-based tourism, such as the 2002 title by McKercher and du Cros quoted on the previous page. Smith's book, published a year later, is a wonderful exploration of political, social, and interpretive issues. Both books include many helpful case studies.

3. **Learn:** *Blue Ridge Heritage Trails.* Heritage trails represent an increasingly popular form of place-based travel. Check out this ambitious initiative, which follows scenic byways through North Carolina, Georgia, Virginia, and Tennessee. A variety of trails, such as "The Blue Ridge Music Trail" and "The Cherokee Heritage Trail," introduce visitors to the region's diverse arts and culture. Many of the same design principles, however, can and should apply locally, whether you're designing a "trail" or not.

4. **Try:** *Place Scan.* When considering an integrated approach to tourism, first identify the members of the "place" sector who provide your community its distinctive character. People jump right away to museums or Main Street programs, which is understandable, but the list is likely longer than you imagine, once you imagine "place" in a more inclusive sense: museums, archaeological sites, military forts and camps, walking tours, historic neighborhoods, landscapes, living history, battlefields, scenic byways, theaters, parks, historic markers, shrines, trails, missions, festivals, farms, zoos, botanical gardens, art districts, cemeteries, National Heritage Areas, cathedrals, and rivers just get the list going. Don't forget restaurants and cafes that serve regional fare, as well as the foods themselves ("culinary tourism"). And then there are the streets, your "outdoor museum": "The streets are clearly places where people engage in the assertion and expression of their culture and identity," writes Melanie Smith in *Issues in Cultural Tourism Studies.* Identify the locations Ray Oldenburg refers to as "great good places" in his book of the same name—places where the public comes together *in community.* Who is helping to tell your story? Bring them together for a preliminary conversation, after distilling the issues here to several core questions, some of which I've provided in the narrative. Take that first step! **Check the recommendations and examples at www.civictourism.org for conducting a "place scan."**

# "FRAME FLIPPING": APPLICATION 1.2
## Beyond a Commodity

*Heritage attractions of the future will be mediators of experience, encouraging postmodern tourists to construct their own sense of history and place, and to create their individual journeys of self-discovery.* ~Szilivia Gymióthy and Nick Johns, "Developing the Role of Quality," in *Quality Issues in Heritage Visitor Attractions*

Civic tourism urges communities to connect to visitors in ways that go beyond a strictly commercial transaction—that is, on personal or even emotional levels. Sam Ham and Betty Weiler write, "The best interpretation engages the visitor both intellectually and emotionally, and is personal, relevant, and meaningful." They are discussing museum exhibitions, but the principle can apply to your downtown, natural wonders, and other place-based attractions. There are many strategies for engaging people in the "meaningful" ways Ham and Weiler recommend, and the good news is some of them are more cost-effective than the alternative. Think about your most memorable vacation experiences: Why do you remember them? Why do you tell others about them?

Why do people, in fact, travel to New Orleans to build homes for Habitat for Humanity? Why do people work in national parks clearing trails? Why do people work alongside archaeologists to help preserve a Zuni site? Why do people do these things on their precious vacation time? Immediately after 9/11, some of the tourism discussion centered on the increased visitation to national parks, the point being that after the attacks vacations to golf courses or mega-malls for some people felt empty, and instead they sought more meaningful experiences.

It is in moments like the Japanese tourist planting a tree in Yosemite that tourism reveals itself as something other than a commodity transaction. In Austin you can adopt a bat living under the Congress Avenue Bridge; you make a commitment to the city, and you *remember* it. Translate that same give-take experience to your planning. Think about the "more than a commodity" experiences your region can provide. Consider that some tourists want to get in touch with something bigger than their day-to-day world; something that provides meaning, connection, and context; something that is comfortable in its own skin—something that belongs.

Place-based tourism products, from a historic district in Nashville to a state park in Wyoming, can inspire a sense of wonder and belonging. Above all they express a story into which you've been invited. Occasionally the story is so old it's incomplete, and it evokes questions people can't help but ask: What would I have done if...? How did they...? Other places—from Pennsylvania's agricultural country to downtown Missoula—inspire statements more than questions: There's health and harmony here. This works.

## "FRAME FLIPPING": APPLICATION 1.2
# 4 To Do: Web, Read, Learn, Try

1. **Web:** *Planeta.com.* Few online resources provide as much information about or insights into place-based tourism as Planeta, which includes posts from scholars around the globe studying issues like "community tourism," as well as stories from practitioners putting theory to work. There's no reason the success stories in places such as Central America or Africa cannot be adapted to towns everywhere.

2. **Read:** *The Ecology of Commerce,* by Paul Hawken. An entrepreneurial businessman, Hawken wrote this book in 1993 to encourage a different role for the marketplace. He asks that we shift our perspective and envision a market that *contributes* to social networks and the natural environment, as opposed to what it often does—the opposite. Although not about tourism, Hawken's argument fits the hospitality industry like a glove: a tourism ethic that helps restore social, built, cultural, and natural landscapes benefits itself by enhancing the very assets it sells.

3. **Learn:** *Ninstints, British Columbia.* In her study *Managing Sacred Sites,* Myra Shackely describes how this Native American coastal village preserves its unique sense of place, providing an experience that goes well beyond a commodity transaction.

4. **Try:** *Place Making.* Different versions of this exercise exist, but essentially you explore with residents the attributes of their town or region that best contribute to the "sense of place" they want to preserve or improve. Some versions send citizens into the community with cameras, so they can photograph favorite "places" and then create a visual map of the community; some exercises incorporate computers loaded with imaging software, allowing participants to do digital storytelling; others develop intricate systems that clump individual preferences into more comprehensive categories so citizens can brainstorm common values or otherwise identify the narratives that connect locations; still others might ask students to write a letter about a favorite part of town for a time capsule. Adapt one of these "visioning" exercises to your tourism agenda, and at least start the conversation: What *is* our "place"? Can it be articulated for tourism development? Should it be? Who says so? **Check the recommendations and examples at www.civictourism.org for conducting a "place making" exercise.**

# "FRAME FLIPPING": APPLICATION 1.3
# Partnerships 101

*Responsibility means working on common tasks even with people who may share little in common with us and, indeed, may have fundamentally different values on some issues.* ~Carmen Sirianni and Lewis Friedland, *Civic Innovation in America*

At the start your committee will want to encourage at least a modest level of collaboration between and among tourism businesses, cultural agencies, land-use groups, local government, and the public.

**1. Serve on Boards:** Cross-pollinate the tourism, heritage, and public sectors. An early step might be to hold a meeting of relevant organizations and urge them all to create a board matrix that mandates diverse talents and connections.

**2. Attend Conferences:** A different board composition is not enough; board members, staff, commissioners, and major donors, for example, should attend and present at one another's conferences. Create a calendar to assure that relevant conferences are not held at the same time, and discuss a theme that each organization might pursue at its annual meeting.

**3. Become Friends:** Most nonprofits have a "Friends" group through which donations can be made. Tourism agencies and chambers of commerce should become Friends. Likewise, the museum should be a member of the chamber. Don't complain that the corporate community doesn't help museums if you don't belong and show up.

**4. Provide Stuff:** Museums often keep 90 percent of their collections in storage. Artifacts that are not priceless can be lent to restaurants, hotels, and other commercial establishments, helping to position the entire town as a "heritage destination" and providing free advertising for museums and other destinations.

**5. Host a Mixer:** Heritage attractions can host an evening reception for tourism employees and their families. One reason motel clerks, for example, don't refer guests to the museum is that they don't know where it is or what it offers. The lodging and restaurant associations should return the favor.

**6. Train Staff:** In collaboration with schools and museums, innovative educational programs teach tourism employees about the history and culture of their community, so they are better prepared to suggest activities to guests.

**7. Lobby Together:** A testimony of a partnership's strength is how well they play together when money is on the table. Ideally, when advocating for tourism appropriations cultural voices should assist, and vice versa. It's shortsighted to view one another as competitors for the same slice of pie; the goal is to increase the pie through partnership.

## "FRAME FLIPPING": APPLICATION 1.3
# 4 To Do: Web, Read, Learn, Try

1. **Web:** *Tourism Ambassador Institute.* Several programs teach hospitality workers about the history and culture of their community. Beyond helping employees deliver quality "customer service," these trainings aim at instilling a sense of pride in place, which visitors readily discern and connect to.

2. **Read:** *Cultural Heritage Tourism: Practical Applications.* This Arizona Humanities Council publication provides numerous tips for strengthening local partnerships. Although the 52-page booklet focuses on heritage tourism, the lessons are applicable to most place-based approaches. Download from www.azhumanities.org.

3. **Learn:** *Public Archaeology in Annapolis.* Parker Potter's 1994 book describes a tourism project that brought residents and visitors together with archaeologists to search for, unearth, and interpret artifacts. The initiative built bonds between cultural and tourism sectors, as well as with residents and guests. Many other communities are using archaeological digs to engage and educate both visitors and residents, helping to build a culture of respect while using tourism as a place-making tool.

4. **Try:** *Heritage Destination.* Create an association of history museums, heritage sites, arts agencies, and environmental groups to provide artifacts for your town's hotel lobbies, restaurants, and store walls—in partnership with the chamber of commerce, for instance. Select a theme related to an upcoming community event and ask each site to contribute objects reflecting the theme. Change the theme in concert with other local events (July 4th, city's birthday, book fair, ethnic festivals). While you're at it, lend objects to City Hall and your legislators' and congresspersons' local offices—artifacts they will walk by everyday, and see your institution's or association's name. **Visit www.civictourism.org for step-by-step recommendations for creating a "heritage destination" program.**

## "RETHINK ECONOMICS": APPLICATION 2.1
# The Triple Bottom Line

*But the notion that we can save the "growth forever" paradigm by dematerializing the economy, or "decoupling" it from resources, or substituting information for resources, is fantasy. We can surely eat lower on the food chain, but we cannot eat recipes!*
~Herman Daly, *Beyond Growth: The Economics of Sustainable Development*

Today, phrases such as "triple bottom line," "sustainable development," and "creative economy" bounce around the halls of business schools at some universities, and the language has certainly caught up to economic development departments at city and state levels. Attend a business conference or pick up an economics journal, and you're likely to find someone talking or writing about these topics. Economic strategy is becoming greener—in the environmental sense, not just the color of money.

That's good news for people who work in museums, preservation programs, arts agencies, environmental organizations, and related place-based institutions, because they represent many of the assets that some observers now recognize as central to quality economic development. It's not just "tree hugging"; there are financial, social, and of course ecological advantages to maintaining healthy forests. The same is true for the other ingredients of place-based tourism.

Which is why trending toward sustainable accounting is welcome news for the hospitality sector: few other industries connect to the elements of triple-bottom-line policy so obviously—in concept and in practice. In fact, if we wanted to design a commercial sector designed specifically for TBL bookkeeping, one would be hard-pressed to find something better than tourism.

**ECONOMIC**
Tourism businesses must earn a profit.
Tourism provides jobs for regions & sectors.
Tourism taxes fund community programs.

**SOCIAL**
Tourism "sells" the places where people live.
Tourism can affect residents more than anyone.
Customers following social & ethical beliefs.

**ENVIRONMENTAL**
More and more the tourism product is the environment (natural & built).
An unsustainable approach can threaten the tourism resource.
More customers want to buy "green."

## "RETHINK ECONOMICS": APPLICATION 2.1
# 4 To Do: Web, Read, Learn, Try

1. **Web:** *Garrett Hardin Society.* Hardin, who died in 2003, is best known for having written "The Tragedy of the Commons," a brief 1968 essay about a grazing meadow, which has been reprinted hundreds of times—in environmental studies, city planning texts, philosophy journals, sociology books, economic treatises, and the literature of most other disciplines. Hardin wrote dozens of books and articles, but he will be remembered for this short piece about "carrying capacity," a concept central to understanding sustainable development and the triple bottom line. A short essay, "The Tragedy of the Commons" would provide for an interesting committee discussion.

2. **Read:** *The Triple Bottom Line,* by Andrew Savitz. Business writer Savitz provides a recent and clear overview of the economic, social, environmental, and philosophical values that underpin triple-bottom-line theory. Filled with dozens of examples that illustrate how companies are incorporating TBL accounting, the book is especially helpful for readers who get blurry-eyed reading economics textbooks. More than a few of the case studies and principles are applicable to tourism development, although Savitz never points this out.

3. **Learn:** *Queen Anne County.* David Edgell, Sr. reports in *Sustainable Tourism: A Legacy for the Future* that Queen Anne County, near Maryland's Chesapeake Bay, is using tourism as a tool to protect the environment. The community understands the importance of tourism, and they have channeled that interest into place-saving strategies that benefit both the fragile wetlands and the economy.

4. **Try:** *TBL Report.* One of the earliest and, in some ways, easiest steps you can take is to design the annual tourism report using triple-bottom-line procedures. In other words, don't simply point out how many people passed through town, how many stayed overnight, how much they spent, and the total tax revenue their activities generated. That's only one sphere of TBL accounting. Also explain the industry's impact on natural and built environments, as well as how tourism affects social networks. Other groups might write these sections (Shell Oil provides space for NGOs to author the environmental part of its annual report). Saying you're going to issue such a report obliges committee members to think about the effects of tourism on all bottom lines, not just *the* bottom line, and doing so mandates partnerships, which, through this single activity, might form the basis for more ambitious activities. Similar to the TBL approach, you might consider adapting the popular "Ecological Footprint" exercise for your tourism report. **Check www.civictourism.org for examples of what a tourism TBL and "ecological footprint" report might look like.**

# "RETHINK ECONOMICS": APPLICATION 2.2
# The New Economy

*[Community leaders] pay lip service to the need to attract talent, but continue to pour resources into underwriting big-box retailers, subsidizing downtown malls, recruiting call centers and squandering precious taxpayer dollars on extravagant stadium complexes. Or they try to create facsimiles of neighborhoods or retail districts, replacing the old and authentic with the new and generic—and in doing so drive the resident Creative Class away.* ~Richard Florida, *The Rise of the Creative Class*

A remarkable thing about New Economy literature—and I'm using the term as a generic place-holder for numerous progressive market policies which, of course, don't always agree—is that much of it ignores the tourism sector. Here are stacks of books prophesying economic trends for the twenty-first century, and they rarely mention what is arguably the largest industry in the world (and perhaps in your town or state).

Whether you accept all of the recommendations from Richard Florida and other economists, I see little to convince me that their premise is inaccurate: authentic, tolerant, culturally vibrant, educationally sound, and environmentally fit places tend to experience stronger economies. Duh. And for those who say they'd *like* to invest in the environment and other "quality" assets, but jobs take precedence—the tired "jobs or the environment" sleight of hand—consider this:

| MYTH: Jobs *or* the environment. | | VS. | REALITY: Jobs *and* the environment. | | |
|---|---|---|---|---|---|
| Strict environmental policies hamper growth and hurt the economy. | | | Environmental protection helps build a stronger economy. | | |
| | Economic Health | Environmental Quality | | Economic Health | Environmental Quality |
| **BOTTOM STATES** Texas | 40 | 49 | **TOP STATES** Hawaii | 1 | 4 |
| Alabama | 46 | 46 | Minnesota | 2 | 7 |
| West Virginia | 48 | 45 | Vermont | 3 | 1 |
| Mississippi | 49 | 43 | New Hampshire | 6 | 2 |
| Louisiana | 50 | 50 | Wisconsin | 9 | 6 |

Source: *Better Not Bigger: How To Take Control of Urban Growth and Improve Your Community*, by Eben Fodor.

### Historic Preservation and Economic Health

"Dollar for dollar, historic preservation is one of the highest job-generating economic development options available. In Michigan, $1,000,000 in building rehabilitation creates 12 more jobs than does manufacturing $1,000,000 of cars. In West Virginia, $1,000,000 of rehabilitation creates 20 more jobs than mining $1,000,000 of coal."

**Investing $1,000,000 in rehabilitation instead of $1,000,000 in new construction results in:**
• an additional $120,000 that stays in the community • 5 to 9 more construction jobs • 4.7 more new jobs elsewhere

Source: *The Economics of Historic Preservation: A Community Leader's Guide*, by Donovan Rypkema.

So, if your tourism is designed, at least in part, around the region's history, culture, or natural environment, why not incorporate the arguments and strategies offered by the New Economy, which encourage cities to *invest* in their place-based stock? Why allow tourism to remain stuck in what Florida calls an industrial-age mindset?

## "RETHINK ECONOMICS": APPLICATION 2.2
# 4 To Do: Web, Read, Learn, Try

1. **Web:** *Creative Class Group.* It's worth perusing Richard Florida's website and blog to familiarize yourself with the literature, read what other communities are doing, and follow online discussions. As you're reading, ask yourself how the underlying principles expressed might apply to local tourism operations.

2. **Read:** *The New Economy of Nature: The Quest To Make Conservation Profitable,* by Gretchen Daily and Katherine Ellison. The authors, one a journalist and the other an ecologist, provide a portrait of innovative projects around the globe that take creative approaches to nature-based economics. Unlike market systems which primarily "use" nature, the transactions here are intended to preserve and improve the environment. Local tourism programs could adopt more than a few of the strategies.

3. **Learn:** *NYC Green Map.* Designed for New Yorkers, the Green Map offers insights for visitors too, showcasing great ways to get around, dine, recreate, live, and work in a "greener" way. Other cities are developing similar tourism tools, both print and online, for the swelling ranks of socially conscious travelers. Consider adding a "green" directory or "green" heritage trail to your tourism website.

4. **Try:** *Creativity Index.* How "creative" is your local economy? Your tourism program? Creativity is about artists, sure, but it's "artists" in the broadest terms—that is, people whose job or lifestyle requires them to think and act creatively: teachers, doctors, lawyers, architects, journalists, CEOs, nonprofit executives, and the like. Richard Florida believes a third of workers falls into this category, and the significant point some cities latch onto is that this group earns more money, thus the desire to recruit the Creative Class. Develop a "creativity index" and conduct a regional survey to evaluate your town's economic infrastructure. It's also possible to apply the same indicators to tourism experiences; that is, are visitors engaged creatively and imaginatively, or are they passively riding along on a dull assembly line, and then departing all too soon? **Check www.civictourism.org for an example of indicators that make up a "creativity index."**

# "RETHINK ECONOMICS": APPLICATION 2.3
## Restorative vs. Wasteful

*If industrial methods of extraction and production under a free-market corporate system are destroying the life around us—and there is no credible evidence to suggest otherwise—then the question is: Can we imagine a market system that achieves exactly the opposite result, that creates, increases, nourishes and enhances life on earth? Can we imagine competition between businesses that improves living and cultural systems?* ~Paul Hawken, *The Ecology of Commerce*

Implicit in triple-bottom-line accounting is the notion of a "restorative" economic system—one that gives back to environmental and social bottom lines, rather than simply exploiting them. As some "natural" economists point out, historically we have treated the environment as "income" without expensing it in ledger books. That's just not sound economic *or* environmental policy. Once it's gone, it's gone, and we cannot create more resources through technological tricks or gimmicky accounting. As Herman Daly says, "More capital does not substitute for less resources, except on a very restricted margin. You cannot make the same house by substituting more saws for less wood."

Like other industrial sectors, tourism has often "used" the ingredients of place—social, environmental, cultural—without returning anything to them and, in fact, some critics argue that an unrestrained hospitality industry corrupts these assets forever. The question Hawken raises above is central to reframing tourism: "Can we imagine a market system that achieves exactly the opposite result, that creates, increases, nourishes and enhances life on earth?" In other words, can we imagine a tourism that leaves us cleaner air, healthier mountains, stronger social networks, better schools and museums, appealing streets—*and* a vibrant economy?

Not only *can* we imagine a restorative tourism, when you consider the alternative it makes little sense for tourism to continue down the "wasteful" path, eventually using up or paving over the very experiences in which it barters. Considered in this way, it's clear that few industries can contribute to or benefit from a healthy triple bottom line as much as tourism.

# "RETHINK ECONOMICS": APPLICATION 2.3
## 4 To Do: Web, Read, Learn, Try

1. **Web:** *Partners for Livable Communities.* PLC is one of several excellent nonprofit organizations that help communities "rethink" what success looks like. In addition to on-the-ground examples that explain how cities and towns are reevaluating economic policies, PLC's library contains publications that survey proven development practices—many designed around cultural assets.

2. **Read:** *Walking the Talk: The Business Case for Sustainable Development,* by Charles Holliday, Jr., Stephan Schmidheiny, and Philip Watts. Written by CEOs of three of the world's largest corporations, and complete with more than sixty best practices worldwide, this book demonstrates that a restorative approach is not only possible, but also imperative. The study is helpful for individual businesses as well as communities hoping to design sustainable practices.

3. **Learn:** *Code of Ethics.* Study the ten-point "Global Code of Ethics for Tourism" adopted by the World Tourism Organization and apply the code to your local tourism operations. Dozens of other sustainability codes, such as the international Earth Charter and Natural Step principles, can also serve as templates. Most tourism codes of conduct are written for the visitor, but creating and monitoring a code encourages the managing organizations to think holistically and long-term. An example can be found in *Amish Country News*, a publication that includes a localized code of ethics covering everything from photographing Amish residents to waving etiquette, and ending with this admonition: "They are not here to serve as tour guides or attractions for visitors. This, after all, is their home, so please respect their beliefs and lifestyle."

4. **Try:** *Restorative Replica.* There is no end to the number of businesses, corporations, governments, and other commercial and public entities that have jumped on the "restorative" and "sustainability" bandwagons. And that's a good thing. Many of these activities have been documented in economic-development literature, such as the book above. From the case studies select a business and trace its evolution from a wasteful to a restorative industry. What were the challenges and how were they overcome? What new systems, departments, and modes of thinking were put in place? What were the benchmarks of success and how were they met? In the end, what were the economic, social, and environmental challenges and *results*, and how were these results measured? You might consider adapting, for example, the Global Reporting Initiative or the CERES Principles, both popular tools that can help measure the tourism industry's social and ecological effects. **Visit www.civictourism.org for an example of a "restorative replica" exercise.**

# "CONNECT TO THE PUBLIC" APPLICATION 3.1
## Saying and Doing

*In a democracy, striking the right balance between communal and market-based values is a task that cannot be delegated to experts. The fundamental judgments must be made by the citizenry or the very idea of democracy is mocked.*
~Daniel Yankelovich, *Coming to Public Judgment*

Some people ask how civic tourism differs from other forms of tourism that encourage community involvement. Geotourism, community tourism, the WTTC's "Blueprint for New Tourism," the National Park Service's gateway communities program, and Agenda 21, for example, all stress "civic engagement." If that weren't enough, here are a few statements from scholars, organizations, and practitioners:

- "Communities should be allowed to decide for themselves how far tourism is a potentially positive development option." ~Melanie K. Smith, *Issues in Cultural Tourism Studies*

- "Tourism development issues should be handled with the participation of concerned citizens." ~Rio Earth Summit

- "Consultation between the tourism industry and local communities ... is essential if they are to work together." ~Tourism Concern

- "No tourism product should be developed or marketed without the involvement and support of the local residents." ~David L. Edgell, Sr., *Managing Sustainable Tourism: A Legacy for the Future*

These are positive statements, so let's acknowledge and build on the advice. Anyone who's worked in the public arena knows, however, it's one thing to say "involve the public" and another to do it. Tourism, in particular, tends to be a topic citizens don't care about; if they do, they're typically locked in a pro-industry "economic development" box or an anti-industry "tourism ruins towns" box. Civic tourism urges communities to adopt deliberative engagement strategies that move participants off their positions toward a shared ethic.

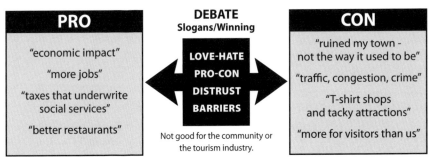

| PRO | DEBATE<br>Slogans/Winning | CON |
|---|---|---|
| "economic impact"<br>"more jobs"<br>"taxes that underwrite social services"<br>"better restaurants" | LOVE-HATE<br>PRO-CON<br>DISTRUST<br>BARRIERS<br><br>Not good for the community or the tourism industry. | "ruined my town - not the way it used to be"<br>"traffic, congestion, crime"<br>"T-shirt shops and tacky attractions"<br>"more for visitors than us" |

# "CONNECT TO THE PUBLIC": APPLICATION 3.1
# 4 To Do: Web, Read, Learn, Try

1. **Web:** *International Association for Public Participation.* Check out IAP2's website, where you'll discover tons of practical advice and links to other organizations that help communities design successful engagement programs. IAP2 conducts conferences and regional workshops that feature scholarly research and practical advice.

2. **Read:** *Tourism: A Community Approach,* by Peter E. Murphy. Written in 1985, Murphy's groundbreaking book is one of the first to argue for citizen participation in formulating tourism policy. Murphy also surveys many programs from around the world experimenting with a civic approach. While the advice is aimed more at tourism scholars and practitioners instead of residents, and while the focus still seems to be on attracting "more" visitors, Murphy's historical analysis of the issues, as well as the possible solutions he discusses, are extremely helpful.

3. **Learn:** *Training Centre for Rural Sustainability.* The "Protected Landscape Approach" encourages citizen participation in and management of cultural landscapes, often for tourism. As documented in *The Protected Landscape Approach*, edited by Jessica Brown, Nora Mitchell, and Michael Beresford, this European training model brings practitioners and citizens together to discuss land-use issues for both cultural preservation and economic development. A similar training institute at the local level would be a welcome addition to place-based tourism planning.

4. **Try:** *Community Scan.* Conduct a community scan, a starting point, to assess what the public knows and thinks about the local tourism industry. Your committee might be surprised. If possible, consult with an outside firm to develop and conduct the survey, so the methodology and interpretation of the findings are not, and do not appear to be, biased. Your town newspaper may run the survey, as might local websites. Among other things, a community scan in which residents are free to self-identify can help you grow the committee. **Check www.civictourism.org for sample "community scan" survey questions and directions.**

# Different Ways Into

*Without active citizens who see in service not the altruism of charity but the responsibility of citizenship on which liberty ultimately depends, no democracy can function properly or, in the long run, even survive.* ~ Benjamin R. Barber, *An Aristocracy of Everyone: The Politics of Education and the Future of America*

Too often our "ways into" a given topic are constructed for us and, beyond that, the discussions are often couched in "either/or" and "black and white" terms. Look at television news: when an issue is introduced the same talking heads from the same newspapers and think tanks beat up one another. In *Culture Wars,* James Hunter refers to this polarizing dynamic as "the discourse of adversaries," which unfortunately still passes for the public's "way into" many issues, including tourism.

Over the past two or three decades studies in sociology, history, politics, journalism, and culture have demonstrated how and why the debate paradigm has generally not benefited the populace—most of whom find themselves somewhere in a messy gray area on many issues. But they rarely see their point of view expressed in the media or popular culture, and their educational systems, political forums, and other social networks often don't provide opportunities to explore, in a democratic and civil fashion, creative ways into a given topic.

Today, organizations such as Study Circles look back to Jefferson's ideal of democracy by the people, the talk-about-it-over-the-fence characteristic Alexis de Tocqueville marveled at in *Democracy in America.* Study Circles and others provide trainings, materials, and methods to help citizens, *as citizens,* discuss tough issues—racism, sprawl, poverty, education, global warming, immigration, and more. Regardless of topic, the deliberative process is usually designed around "choice making"—that is, laying out possibilities in a complete and balanced way, digging beneath the values that define each choice, and reaching a direction with which most people can live. In discussing potential tourism actions, the same methods can and should be applied. Once you understand the deliberative pattern, information flows and designs emerge, and you really *can* encourage a different and more productive conversation about tourism.

# 4 To Do: Web, Read, Learn, Try

1. **Web:** *Study Circles Resource Center.* Your library may lend Study Circles materials, or perhaps a nearby school uses the program; still, visit the website as well to get a sense of the "deliberative" as opposed to "debate" paradigm. When designing public meetings to discuss tourism operations, one goal is to put "choice making" in the hands of the public, not the experts, and the Study Circles philosophy can help create that approach.

2. **Read:** *Practical Politics: Five Principles for a Community That Works,* by Michael Briand. Longtime engagement scholar Briand provides a handful of useful suggestions for designing public activities that produce community buy-in and a shared approach to dicey problems. Briand stresses the "values" dimension of community conversations, an important part of any tourism discussion designed around place, because it is a concept absolutely grounded in and defined by values.

3. **Learn:** *Queensland Ecotourism Plan.* As David Weaver reports in *Ecotourism,* Australia arguably leads the world in its proactive, community-based approach to alternative tourism. The Queensland Ecotourism Plan, adopted in 1997, includes four key strategies, one of them being "Community Development," which, among other roles, involves citizens in "assessing and monitoring local socio-cultural impacts" of tourism. The engagement strategy has different levels, from structured partnerships involving Aboriginal communities to educational efforts that reach the broader community.

4. **Try:** *Choice Making.* Buy or borrow a copy of a National Issues Forum (NIF) reader from the Kettering Foundation (order online or possibly find it at your library). Note how NIF materials present an issue so as to encourage choice-making by the general public—presenting three or four "options," each of which is described in a complete and fair manner, is framed around "values" as well as facts, provides a historical and social perspective, comments on and distinguishes itself from the other options, and helps create a larger context for conversation. Work with your committee to develop a similar "way into" a topical tourism discussion, perhaps a public controversy about widening a road to accommodate more visitor traffic. Even before the publication is shared with the larger public, putting the reader together will be an education itself for your committee. Then test the discussion format with a focus group using a trained NIF discussion leader (check with Kettering or a college or university). Redesign it and roll it out to the public as an early committee project. **Visit www.civictourism.org for an example of how "choice-making" strategies can be applied to tourism discussions.**

# "CONNECT TO THE PUBLIC": APPLICATION 3.3
## The Public as Advocates

*In the process, the entrepreneurship of power, never far from what politics must always be, becomes less self-centered; more politicians come to see it not as a zero-sum game where whatever power you have is power I lack, but instead as an expanding sum, the whole city can grow stronger, healthier, and in every sense more prosperous.*
~ Daniel Kemmis, *The Good City and the Good Life: Renewing the Sense of Community*

When tourism offices put together speakers bureaus and other tools to engage the public, they generally have one purpose: to convince residents that tourism is a wonderful industry. The one-way message goes something like: The industry provides jobs; locals wouldn't have wonderful restaurants and other attractions without tourism; and every dollar invested in travel marketing returns six, eight, or ten times that amount to the public coffers.

It's a familiar and important story told in every bureau's publications, on websites, and before city councils and legislative committees. And it's often ineffective with the public, because we're talking *at* people rather than engaging them. In fact, some residents see tourism as antithetical to healthy place-making, so when industry officials lobby few "regular" voices join them. Elected officials expect the manager of a hotel or president of the restaurant association to testify for tourism funding. What's often as effective is the voice of a schoolteacher or librarian. Why?

- They don't represent a special interest and thus their testimony is considered impartial and more meaningful.

- They represent "white hat" organizations (schools, libraries) that almost everyone values.

- Tourism is a mobile industry and your hotel manager may have just arrived. Longtime residents, on the other hand, often went to school with their legislators, they know one another's families, they're on a first-name basis.

- Most elected officials are proud of their districts. When they give speeches they often begin by mentioning their mountains, cultures, and history. Tap into that. Having a teacher explain why and how tourism is helping to preserve traditions lends more credibility to the argument.

Begin by demonstrating to residents that they *have* a voice in tourism planning. Next, stop talking about tourism as gift shops, motels, and restaurants. Your museum and library are connected to tourism, even if they're not "attractions." For instance, assume 10 percent of your state budget is generated by tourism spending; imagine lopping 10 percent from every agency that receives state funding—museums, libraries, social services, schools. But shift your language from economics toward the services provided. Don't read a spreadsheet. Tell a story.

## "CONNECT TO THE PUBLIC": APPLICATION 3.3
# 4 To Do: Web, Read, Learn, Try

1. **Web:** *National Trust for Historic Preservation.* Consult NTHP's website for information about historic preservation and heritage tourism, but also for advocacy advice. The Trust is involved with governments at all levels; learn from their experiences and consult their library of materials that walk communities through the advocacy maze. Yes, the Trust has strong leadership at the top, but its success is equally due to strong connections at the local level. Additionally, the Trust's *Share Your Heritage* publication is a particularly helpful survey of cultural heritage tourism best practices, occasionally describing the political contexts and advocacy work.

2. **Read:** *The Economics of Historic Preservation: A Community Leader Guide.* Preservation advocate Donovan Rypkema, manager of the consulting firm PlaceEconomics, provides communities with ample ammunition to develop an advocacy campaign. Many arguments Rypkema suggests for saving historic structures can be applied to cultural and environmental issues as well. The facts and numbers support a responsible tourism ethic, as does the personal element. Marshal the quantitative and qualitative arguments, educate the public, generate support, and move on!

3. **Learn:** *Scotland Land Purchases.* Some communities have joined forces to become extremely proactive politically. Scotland, for example, allows for and supplements community buy-outs of land, in order to position the resource for tourism and broader economic development activities. On the Stòras Uibhist website the island's tourism committee writes, "We believe that the community ownership of South Uist, Benbecula, and Eriskay presents us with a unique opportunity to develop appropriately the resources that we have."

4. **Try:** *Lobbyist.* Groups often shy away from hiring a professional, thinking that they know the facts better and can make the case themselves, or that lobbying is oily and they don't want to besmirch their good name, or that they simply don't have the resources. Consider hiring, on a short-term basis, a professional to meet with your committee and the public to at least get an outsider's view of the issues, possibilities, and strategies. Pull the public into advocacy work from the beginning; don't turn to them at the eleventh hour and ask for phone calls to your legislator. **Visit www.civictourism.org for a sample advocacy campaign—timelines, benchmarks, strategies.**

## "INVEST IN THE STORY": APPLICATION 4.1
# Place at the Nexus

*What every community needs, in other words, is a systematic assessment of is own landscape character, an inventory of the connectedness it has—and of any broken connections that need mending.* ~Tony Hiss, *The Experience of Place*

As Hiss hints at in this passage, and as civic tourism emphasizes, "place" is about *connectedness*, the ways in which cultural, natural, and built environments relate to one another, shed light on each other, and help round out the local "story." In towns and cities a vibrant sense of place often exists in the sweet spot where the different environments come together.

## INTEGRATED STORIES = "PLACE"

What does the streetscape reveal about a community's history or values?

CULTURAL HERITAGE

HISTORIC PRESERVATION

What role did nature play in local history?

NATURE

How does the natural setting affect the built environment?

Consequently, groups working to preserve natural, cultural, and built environments should collaborate in order to "write" a thorough community narrative. Give visitors something to read. When I leave your town, can I say why you exist, what your political and social persuasions are, and what you value as the most important chapters of your story? Try this: Select a handful of place-based assets and discuss how they might be repackaged and reinterpreted to create Hiss's "inventory of... connectedness"—say, the history museum, wilderness area, art district, and historic neighborhood. Think ecologically: How do the pieces fit together? What does each say about the others? What do your streets, for example, tell guests about community values toward the natural environment? In *Great Streets*, Allan Jacobs writes that streets "represent a public memory." What do yours say the public remembers? Think of your town as a museum. Tell the story.

# 4 To Do: Web, Read, Learn, Try

1. **Web:** *Center for Sustainable Destinations.* Managed by *National Geographic*, this site discusses the principles and practices of geotourism, an international effort that has spearheaded some of the civic and interpretive concepts emphasized here. Use the community-building ethics implicit in geotourism to uncover the complete "place thing."

2. **Read:** *The Ecology of Place: Planning for Environment, Economy, and Community,* by Timothy Beatley and Kristy Manning. Few books provide as clear a historical, social, and environmental analysis of "sense of place." This book should be on every city planner's bookshelf; it will cause you to look at and value your town differently.

3. **Learn:** *The Delphi Technique.* In *Tourism and Sustainability*, Mowforth and Munt describe a strategy used to identify and position place for tourism development by establishing carrying capacity thresholds. The Delhi Technique measures physical, social, and economic factors in order to calculate acceptable levels of change or development.

4. **Try:** *Nexus World.* It's all well and good to talk about the ingredients of place "shedding light on one another" and "rounding out the story," but how does that happen? Try this exercise with a group of students, divided into the following clusters: art, land, finances, people, events. Select a historic building in town and ask each group to research, through oral histories, Internet searches, and the library, the historic structure from their cluster's perspective. For example, the "art" committee can study the building's architecture, investigate the art displayed in the building, research artists who may have lived there, describe how the building does or doesn't contribute to the city design, and so on. Then overlay the clusters and look for patterns—the ways they do and don't work together. Do that enough and a story emerges that uncovers a community's values and informs planning. **Visit www.civictourism.org for additional "nexus world" exercises.**

# Authenticity

*And now we are beginning to see simulations of simulations. For example, the new Sega theme park in London will offer simulated (via virtual reality) rides of an already simulated ride in, say, Disney World.* ~George Ritzer and Allan Liska, "McDisneyization and Post-tourism," in *Touring Cultures: Transformations of Travel and Theory*

Attend any discussion of place-based tourism and two words will likely pop up: "authenticity" and "quality." Most people recognize that "quality" is, like "beauty," a fluid, relativistic, and personal concept that changes depending on different contexts and perspectives. "Authenticity," on the other hand, is sometimes talked about as if it's an unequivocal standard, but ask what it means and you may hear, "Your project should be real and complete." First, there's considerable debate as to whether tourists, especially "post-tourists," really want the authentic. Beyond that, your presentation is *never* real and complete. All presentations, argues Chris Rojek in *Touring Cultures,* are to an extent inauthentic and contrived. If that weren't enough, here are a few other voices on "authenticity":

- "Authenticity is a 'socially constructed concept' and the meaning is negotiable." ~Eric Cohen
- "Authenticity is neither a unified static construct nor an essential property of objects and events." ~Tazim Jamal and S. Hall
- "The notion that authenticity is a concept which is open to various interpretations and experience is crucial, for it then informs our discussion of the nature of commodification of culture." ~Siobhan Drummond
- "An authentic culture is not one that remains unchanged, which seems impossible under any condition, but one that retains the ability to determine the appropriateness of its adaptations." ~Betty Duggan
- "Authenticity is not an objective phenomenon but, rather, authenticity is a 'negotiable concept' which is open to change." ~Kathryn Burnett

When tourists attend a Native American dance and are not shown the "real" ceremony for religious reasons, are they seeing an "authentic" performance? Is there such a thing, as Dean MacCannell says, as "staged authenticity" and is that okay? Who says? In your place-based deliberations, the "authenticity" shadow is certain to lurk about, rightfully so. Through conversation you may discover that authenticity

| Does Not Always Mean... | Can Mean... | Probably Should Mean... |
|---|---|---|
| • Stuffy and boring | • Entertaining, fun, enjoyable | • Tell the story, not the photo-op |
| • Complete | • Relevant, connected to viewers | • Dispel myths and stereotypes |
| • Static and unchanged history | • "Staged" (MacCannell) | • Don't knowingly misrepresent |
| | | • Always being reinterpreted |

# 4 To Do: Web, Read, Learn, Try

1. **Web:** *American Association for State and Local History.* One of many national history associations, AASLH regularly conducts workshops and trainings for people doing the work of local history. Check their programs and publications sections in particular; some activities and book titles deal with the authenticity issue.

2. **Read:** *Authenticity: What Consumers Really Want,* by James H. Gilmore and B. Joseph Pine II. More business-oriented than cultural, this recent publication by the authors of *The Experience Economy* discusses the fickle concept called authenticity, which nearly every place-based tourism program argues is essential. But what *is* it and how do we deliver it, in products and services?

3. **Learn:** *New Key to Costa Rico.* Monitoring and accreditation programs have proliferated, especially since place-based tourism has become more popular. How do you know the history is accurate? How do you know your trip to a nature preserve does not damage the environment? *New Key* is one of the earliest guidebooks, letting visitors know if their Costa Rico trip is authentic ecotourism or if it's "eco-lite."

4. **Try:** *Authenticity.* Many authenticity exercises exist, and tackling them as a citizens' committee will illustrate just how prickly place-making can be. For example, consider the controversy that erupted in Colonial Williamsburg when the living history site reenacted a slave auction. On one hand it is historically accurate, that is, "authentic," to say such auctions took place during the colonial era, and some historians believe the auctions illustrate just how degrading slavery is. On the other hand, some people feel the entertainment aspect trivializes the reality, while others say the reenactments are degrading to African American viewers. **You can find this and other "authenticity" exercises at www.civictourism.org.**

## "INVEST IN THE STORY": APPLICATION 4.3
# The Missing Link

*The most pressing and imminent danger is the conventional wisdom, at least among decision makers, that investment in heritage—or culture in general—must inevitably be beneficial to both economic development and heritage resources by directly or indirectly producing a profitable return to each.* ~Brian Graham, G. J. Ashworth, and J. E. Turnbridge, *A Geography of Heritage: Power, Culture & Economy*

The typical "tourism agency," whether local or state, devotes the majority of its energy, time, and budget to the top half of the circle below. They're advertisers, often very good at what they do, and the best undertake a great deal of research and development to support their marketing mission. The place community should support their efforts and help increase appropriations. And vice versa. Although some tourism programs use "product development" language, with few exceptions that generally doesn't translate to significant funding for place-based attractions, which is what's *really* needed, not more studies, marketing, or pats on the back.

What resources *do* exist are few, they're episodic and project-centered, they tend to reinforce silo thinking, and they rarely have anything to do with tourism. Compared to the way states approach travel *marketing*, there is no concerted place-based tourism *development* effort upon which communities can rely. That's a missing link in most local tourism operations, but if that link is forged, the bond can strengthen both the marketing sector, because they have a better product to sell, and the place community, pulling them together around a common cause.

**Where Is Product Development Now?**

**Scattered:**
• Local • State • Federal • Some Private

**Silos:**
• Land • Buildings • Cultural

• **No coordinated vision.**
• **Few tourismspecific programs.**
• **Few long-term opportunities.**
• **Difficult for rural.**

That "development" is conceptual *and* financial, and the money part is not just tossing dollars at museums and other institutions. It's also resources that support planning and help build capacity, so communities are prepared to use product funding competently; it's support that mandates partnerships between cultural, business, and planning sectors, so the community moves forward together; and it's encouragement to continually upgrade and monitor place-making activities.

## "INVEST IN THE STORY": APPLICATION 4.3
# 4 To Do: Web, Read, Learn, Try

1. **Web:** *Connecticut's Heritage Gateway: Cultural Heritage Development Fund.* Managed by the Connecticut Humanities Council, this program provides funds for heritage and cultural organizations to plan, build, and maintain place-based products that serve the state's tourism effort. One of the earliest investment models, a similar program would be a welcome addition in any region.

2. **Read:** *The Tourist City,* edited by Dennis R. Judd and Susan S. Fainstein. Primarily focused on well-known tourism towns throughout the world (Las Vegas, Budapest, Boston, etc.), this anthology also raises investment questions: How are tourism programs thought through and paid for? What innovative funding schemes have cities created to build and sustain attractions?

3. **Learn:** *Iowa Great Places.* One of a handful of programs that pull together various state agencies to assist communities with place-making for tourism development, "Iowa Great Places" provides planning funds, capacity-building support, and project-related assistance. Dozens of towns have completed the program.

4. **Try:** *Local Tourism History.* Here's a way to blend the cultural and tourism soup of this conversation, a project that could be an early get-to-know-you activity *and* something of value for the future. Tourism has written an important chapter in the history of many communities, but few places have a copy of that document. Partner with a high school to research the tourism story through student research—oral histories, Internet, libraries. A few states have Heritage Projects, affiliates of the American Folklife Center of the U.S. Library of Congress, that partner with schools, sending students into the community to conduct the kind of research just mentioned. Partner with them if possible. Old-timers, in particular, will tell you about how society *was*, about how streets *were*, and you begin to appreciate how much tourism, if at all, has come to define the changes. That'll be a story the cultural folks can add to their museums and interpretive sites, the tourism crowd can add to its corporate identity and use the research as a tool for planning and advocacy, and the designers of economic policy can study.

# WORKS
# REFERENCED

In order to avoid constantly interrupting the conversations, I have not used footnotes or other citations. Quotations and other references in the narrative are taken from the following works. Visit the bibliography at www.civictourism.org for annotated descriptions of these and related publications. Consider a book-discussion activity with your tourism committee and the community; your library or museum may help sponsor it.

Abbey, Edward. "Industrial Tourism." *Desert Solitaire: A Season in the Wilderness*. New York: Ballantine Books, 1968.

Allen, Paula Gunn. "The Sacred Hoop: A Contemporary Perspective." *The Ecocriticism Reader: Landmarks in Literary Ecology*, ed. Cheryll Glotfelty and Harold Fromm. Athens: University of Georgia Press, 1996.

Austin, Mary. *The Land of Little Rain*. New York: Modern Library, 2003.

Bachelard, Gaston. *The Poetics of Space*. Boston: Beacon Press, 1958.

Barber, Benjamin R. *An Aristocracy of Everyone: The Politics of Education and the Future of America*. New York: Oxford University Press, 1994.

Beatley, Timothy, and Kristy Manning. *The Ecology of Place: Planning for Environment, Economy, and Community*. Washington, D.C.: Island Press, 1997.

Bellah, Robert, et al. *Habits of the Heart: Individualism and Commitment in American Life*. New York: Harper & Row, 1985.

Berry, Wendell. *Home Economics*. San Francisco: North Point Press, 1987.

———. *What Are People For?* San Francisco: North Point Press, 1990.

Bird, Isabella. *A Lady's Life in the Rocky Mountains*. Norman: University of Oklahoma Press, 1999.

Boniface, Priscilla. *Managing Quality Cultural Tourism*. London: Routledge, 1995.

Bosselman, Fred P., Craig A. Peterson, and Claire McCarthy. *Managing Tourism Growth: Issues and Applications*. Washington, D.C.: Island Press, 1999.

Briand, Michael. *Practical Politics: Five Principles for a Community That Works*. Urbana: University of Illinois Press, 1999.

Brooks, David. *BOBOS in Paradise: The New Upper Class and How They Got There*. New York: Simon & Schuster, 2000.

Brown, Jessica, Nora Mitchell, and Michael Beresford, eds. *The Protected Landscape Approach: Linking Nature, Culture and Community*. Gland, Switzerland: World Conservation Union, 2005.

Carson, Rachel. *Silent Spring*. New York: Houghton Mifflin, 1962.

Castaneda, Carlos. *The Teachings of Don Juan: A Yaqui Way of Knowledge*. New York: Pocket Books, 1974.

Cather, Willa. *Death Comes for the Archbishop*. New York: Alfred A. Knopf, 1927.

Chambers, Erve, ed. *Tourism and Culture: An Applied Perspective*. Albany: State University of New York Press, 1997.

Coupland, Douglas. *Shampoo Planet*. London: Simon & Schuster, 1993.

Cronon, William, ed. *Uncommon Ground: Rethinking the Human Place in Nature*. New York: Norton, 1996.

Daily, Gretchen C., and Katherine Ellison. *The New Economy of Nature: The Quest To Make Conservation Profitable*. Washington, D.C.: Island Press, 2002.

Daly, Herman. *Beyond Growth: The Economics of Sustainable Development*. Boston: Beacon Press, 1996.

Davidson, Eric A. *You Can't Eat GNP: Economics As If Ecology Mattered*. Cambridge, Mass.: Perseus, 2000.

Diamond, Jared. *Collapse: How Societies Choose to Fail or Succeed*. New York: Viking, 2005.

Dillard, Annie. *Pilgrim at Tinker Creek*. Cutchogue, N.Y.: Buccaneer Books, 1974.

Duany, Andres, Elizabeth Plater-Zyberk, and Jeff Speck. *Suburban Nation: The Rise of Sprawl and the Decline of the American Dream*. New York: North Point Press, 2000.

Edwards, Andres R. *The Sustainability Revolution: Portrait of a Paradigm Shift*. Gabriola Island, B.C.: New Society Publishers, 2005.

Elkington, John. *Cannibals with Forks: The Triple Bottom Line of 21st Century Business*. Philadelphia: New Society, 1998.

Edgell, Sr., David L. *Managing Sustainable Tourism: A Legacy for the Future*. Binghamton, N.Y.: The Haworth Press, 2006.

Elton, Charles. *Animal Ecology*. New York: Macmillan, 1927.

Esty, Daniel C., and Andrew S. Winston. *Green to Gold: How Smart Companies Use Environmental Strategy to Innovate, Create Value, and Build Competitive Advantage*. New Haven: Yale University Press, 2006.

Everden, Neil. "Beyond Ecology: Self, Place, and the Pathetic Fallacy." *The Ecotourism Reader: Landmarks in Literary Ecology*, ed. Cheryll Glotfelty and Harold Fromm. Athens: University of Georgia Press, 1996.

Feifer, Maxine. *Tourism in History: From Imperial Rome to the Present*. New York: Stein and Day, 1985.

Florida, Richard. *The Flight of the Creative Class: The New Global Competition for Talent*. New York: HarperCollins, 2005.

———. *The Rise of the Creative Class: And How It's Transforming Work, Leisure, Community and Everyday Life*. New York: Basic Books, 2002.

Fodor, Eben. *Better Not Bigger: How To Take Control of Urban Growth and Improve Your Community*. Gabriola Island, B.C.: New Society Publishers, 1999.

Galbraith, John Kenneth. *The Affluent Society*. New York: New American Library, 1958.

Garreau, Joel. *Edge City: Life on the New Frontier*. New York: Anchor Books, 1991.

Goeldner, Charles R., and J. R. Brent Ritchie. *Tourism: Principles, Practices, Philosophies*, 9th ed. Hoboken, N.J.: John Wiley & Sons, 2003.

Graham, Brian, G. J. Ashworth, and J. E. Tunbridge. *A Geography of Heritage: Power, Culture and Economy*. London: Arnold, 2000.

Gratz, Roberta B. *Cities Back from the Edge: New Life for Downtown*. New York: John Wiley & Sons, 1998.

Gymióthy, Szilivia, and Nick Johns, "Developing the Role of Quality," *Quality Issues in Heritage Visitor Attractions*, ed. Siobhan Drummond and Ian Yeoman. Oxford: Butterworth-Heinemann, 2001.

Hardin, Garrett. "Tragedy of the Commons." *Science*, 1968.

Harris, Rob, Tony Griffin, and Peter Williams, eds. *Sustainable Tourism: A Global Perspective*. Oxford: Butterworth-Heinemann, 2002.

Hart, Stuart L. *Capitalism at the Crossroads: Aligning Business, Earth, and Humanity*, 2nd ed. Upper Saddle River, N.J.: Wharton School Publishing, 2007.

Hawken, Paul. *The Ecology of Commerce: A Declaration of Sustainability*. New York: HarperCollins, 1993.

Hawken, Paul, Amory Lovins, and L. Hunter Lovins. *Natural Capitalism: Creating the Next Industrial Revolution*. Boston: Little, Brown, 1999.

Hewison, Robert. *The Heritage Industry: Britain in a Climate of Decline*. London: Methuen, 1987.

Hiss, Tony. *The Experience of Place*. New York: Knopf, 1990.

Holliday, Jr., Charles O., Stephan Schmidheiny, and Philip Watts. *Walking the Talk: The Business Case for Sustainable Development*. Sheffield, UK: Greenleaf Publishing Unlimited, 2002.

Honey, Martha. *Ecotourism and Sustainable Development: Who Owns Paradise?* Washington, D.C.: Island Press, 1999.

Howkins, John. *The Creative Economy: How People Make Money from Ideas*. New York: Penguin, 2002.

Hunter, James Davison. *Culture Wars: The Struggle to Define America*. New York: BasicBooks, 1991.

Ishiguro. Kazuo. *Never Let Me Go*. New York: Vintage, 2005.

Jackson, Kenneth T. *Crabgrass Frontier: The Suburbanization of the United States*. New York: Oxford University Press, 1985.

Jacobs, Allan. *Great Streets*. Cambridge: MIT Press, 1993.

Jacobs, Jane. *The Death and Life of Great American Cities*. New York: Random House, 1961.

Judd, Dennis R., and Susan S. Fainstein. *The Tourist City*. New Haven: Yale University Press, 1999.

Kay, Jane Holtz. *Asphalt Nation: How the Automobile Took Over America and How We Can Take It Back.* Berkeley: University of California Press, 1997.

Kemmis, Daniel. *The Good City and the Good Life: Renewing the Sense of Community.* New York: Houghton Mifflin, 1995.

Kirshenblatt-Gimblett, Barbara. *Destination Culture: Tourism, Museums, and Heritage.* Berkeley: University of California Press, 1998.

Krutch, Joseph Wood. *The Desert Year.* Tucson: University of Arizona Press, 1951.

Kunstler, James Howard. *The Geography of Nowhere: The Rise and Decline of America's Man-Made Landscapes.* New York: Simon & Schuster, 1993.

Lakoff, George. *Don't Think of an Elephant!* White River Junction, Vt.: Chelsea Green Publishing, 2004.

Leopold, Aldo. *A Sand County Almanac.* New York: Ballantine Books, 1949.

Lippard, Lucy R. *The Lure of the Local: Senses of Place in a Multicentered Society.* New York: The New Press, 1997.

———. *On the Beaten Track: Tourism, Art, and Place.* New York: The New Press, 1999.

MacCannell, Dean. *The Tourist: A New Theory of the Leisure Class.* 3rd ed. Berkeley: University of California Press, 1999.

MacKaye, Benton. *The New Exploration: A Philosophy of Regional Planning.* Urbana: University of Illinois Press, 1962.

Maclean, Norman. *A River Runs Through It and Other Stories.* Chicago: University of Chicago Press, 1976.

Masumoto, David Mas. *Epitaph for a Peach: Four Seasons on My Family Farm.* New York: HarperCollins, 1995.

Mathews, David. *Politics for People: Finding a Responsible Public Voice.* Urbana: University of Illinois Press, 1994.

McKercher, Bob, and Hilary du Cros. *Cultural Tourism: The Partnership Between Tourism and Heritage Management.* Binghamton, NY.: Haworth Hospitality Press, 2002.

Molotch, Harvey. "The City as a Growth Machine: Toward a Political Economy of Place." *American Journal of Sociology,* 1976.

Mowforth, Martin, and Ian Munt. *Tourism and Sustainability: New Tourism in the Third World.* London: Routledge, 1998.

Mumford, Lewis. *The City in History: Its Origins, Its Transformations, and Its Prospects.* San Diego: Harcourt, 1961.

Murphy, Peter E. *Tourism: A Community Approach.* London: Routledge, 1985.

Nash, Roderick. *The Rights of Nature: A History of Environmental Ethics.* Madison: University of Wisconsin Press, 1989.

Oldenburg, Ray. *The Great Good Place: Cafes, Coffee Shops, Community Centers, Beauty Parlors, General Stores, Bars, Hangouts, and How They Get You Through the Day.* New York: Paragon House, 1989.

Perkins, John. *Confessions of an Economic Hit Man.* New York: Plume, 2004.

Pink, Daniel. *A Whole New Mind: Why Right-Brainers Will Rule the Future.* New York: Berkley Publishing Group, 2005.

Pollan, Michael. *Second Nature: A Gardener's Education.* New York: Atlantic Monthly Press, 1991.

Pope, Alexander. "Epistle IV: Hard Boyle, Earl of Burlington." *The Poetical Works of Alexander Pope.* London: Elibron Classics, 2006.

Porritt, Jonathon. *Capitalism As If the World Matters.* London: Earthscan Publications, 2005.

Putnam, Robert. *Bowling Alone: The Collapse and Revival of American Community.* New York: Simon & Schuster, 2000.

Ray, Paul H., and Sherry Ruth Anderson, *The Cultural Creatives: How 50 Million People Are Changing the World.* New York: Three Rivers Press, 2000.

Robinson, John P., and Geoffrey Godbey. *Time for Life: The Surprising Ways Americans Use Their Time*. University Park: Pennsylvania State University Press, 1997.

Rojek, Chris, and John Urry, eds. *Touring Cultures: Transformations of Travel and Theory*. London: Routledge, 1997.

Rothman, Hal, ed. *The Culture of Tourism, the Tourism of Culture: Selling the Past to the Present in the American Southwest*. Albuquerque: University of New Mexico Press, 2003.

Rothman, Hal. *Devil's Bargains: Tourism in the Twentieth-Century American West*. Lawrence: University Press of Kansas, 1998.

Rybczynski, Witold. *City Life*. New York: Simon & Schuster, 1995.

———. *A Clearing in the Distance: Frederick Law Olmstead and America in the 19th Century*. New York: Touchstone, 1999.

Rypkema, Donovan. *The Economics of Historic Preservation: A Community Leader's Guide*. Washington, D.C.: The National Trust for Historic Preservation, 1994.

Sanders, Scott Russell. *Staying Put: Making a Home in a Restless World*. Boston: Beacon Press, 1993.

Savitz, Andrew. *The Triple Bottom Line*. San Francisco: John Wiley & Sons, 2006.

Schneider, Anne Larason, and Helen Ingram. *Policy Design for Democracy*. Lawrence: University of Kansas Press, 1997.

Schor, Juliet. *The Overworked American: The Unexpected Decline of Leisure*. New York: Basic Books, 1992.

Schumacher, E. F. *Small Is Beautiful: Economics as if People Mattered*. New York: Harper & Row, 1973.

Sen, Amartya. *Development as Freedom*. New York: Anchor Books, 1999.

Silko, Leslie Marmon. *Ceremony*. New York: Viking, 1977.

Sirianni Carmen, and Lewis Friedland, *Civic Innovation in America: Community Empowerment, Public Policy, and the Movement for Civic Renewal*. Berkeley: University of California Press, 2001.

Smith, Melanie K. *Issues in Cultural Tourism Studies*. London: Routledge, 2003.

Snyder, Gary. *Turtle Island*. New York: New Directions, 1969.

Stegner, Wallace. *The Sound of Mountain Water: The Changing American West*. New York: Doubleday, 1969.

———. *Where the Bluebird Sings to the Lemonade Springs: Living and Writing in the West*. New York: Penguin, 1992.

Thoreau, Henry David. *Walden and Other Writings of Henry David Thoreau*, ed. Brooks Atkinson. New York: Modern Library, 1937.

Virgil. *The Georgics*. New York: Oxford University Press, 2006.

Weaver, David. *Ecotourism*. Sydney: John Wiley & Sons, 2001.

———. *Sustainable Tourism: Theory and Practice*. Oxford: Elsevier Butterworth-Heinemann, 2006.

Williams, Terry Tempest. *Refuge: An Unnatural History of Family and Place*. New York: Vintage, 1991.

Withey, Lynne. *Grand Tours and Cook's Tours: A History of Leisure Travel, 1750–1915*. New York: William Morrow, 1997.

Worster, Donald. *A River Running West: The Life of John Wesley Powell*. New York: Oxford University Press, 2001.

———. *The Wealth of Nature*. Oxford: Oxford University Press, 1993.

Yankelovich, Daniel. *Coming to Public Judgment: Making Democracy Work in a Complex World*. Syracuse: Syracuse University Press, 1991.

Zander, Rosamund Stone. *The Art of Possibility: Transforming Professional and Personal Life*. New York: Penguin, 2000.

# ACKNOWLEDGMENTS

Two institutions underwrote and otherwise supported most of the research and public programming for the civic tourism project. The Institute of Museum and Library Services (IMLS), a federal agency, provided a major grant that provided for dozens of public forums, statewide meetings, and a national conference to discuss the issues embedded in a civic approach to tourism development. I thank IMLS for its support of an idea, one that grew and evolved considerably as the project progressed. Secondly, Sharlot Hall Museum in Prescott, Arizona, was the project headquarters for more than two years. There probably aren't too many other heritage sites that practice the principles of civic tourism in a more appropriate and successful way than Sharlot Hall Museum, and I thank the museum's talented staff and board of directors for their generous commitment to the conversation. I especially want to acknowledge the institution's former director, Richard Sims, now executive director of the Montana Historical Society, whose vision and civic-mindedness are reflected on nearly every page of this publication.

Other organizations offered valuable support as well. Tourism Cares for Tomorrow provided funding for the March 2006 national conference. I especially want to recognize the Arizona Humanities Council (AHC), whose early research into cultural and heritage tourism, much of it also underwritten by IMLS with support from the Museum Association of Arizona, provided a starting point for civic tourism. AHC's director, Julie Yoder, read much of this manuscript and offered constructive recommendations. Thanks to the School of Community Resources and Development at Arizona State University for providing a research intern, and even more thanks to that intern, Tiffani Borcherding, for her immeasurable contributions. Dozens of museums, heritage sites, government agencies, and tourism bureaus around Arizona held community workshops, attended statewide summits, and participated in other research and program activities. I particularly want to thank Allan Affeldt, Mayor of Winslow; Roger Beadle, Yuma Chamber of Commerce; Ruth Brydon, Lake Havasu City Museum; Julie Brooks, Wickenburg Chamber of Commerce; Stacey Button, Flagstaff Chamber of Commerce; Karen Churchard, Arizona Tourism Alliance; Kathy Davis, Montezuma National Park; Carrie Gustavson, Bisbee Mining and History Museum; Roger Lidman, Pueblo Grande Museum; Jo Ann Stuckey, Cave Creek Museum; and Janeen Trevillyan, Sedona History Museum. Joanna Smith worked diligently on the project's video and DVD components, as did Ericka and Ryan Wood on the civic tourism website and this publication.

Dozens more people deserve recognition, but I have space for a handful: Scott Russell Sanders' commitment to place weaves its way throughout his many publications, and I thank Scott for his friendship, as well as his generous and ongoing contribution to our work in Arizona. Four people keynoted the project's early statewide summits and helped push the conversation to a new level: Bruce Fraser, director of the Connecticut Humanities Council; David Weaver, professor of tourism at the University of South Carolina; Amy Webb of the National Trust for Historic Preservation; and Deborah Witte from the Kettering Foundation. Special thanks to the dozens of presenters and hundreds of participants who attended the 2006 national conference, which we thought was the culminating activity but in many ways became a new beginning. Immense gratitude as well to Mark McDermott, a career tourism professional and former director of the Arizona Office of Tourism. Mark has taught me more about the industry than any stack of books I might read, and he co-presented with me at most community forums. For more than a decade, I've benefited from summers reading and writing in the hills of Montana, a sanctuary provided by two generations of the family Doggett. Much appreciation to Jamie, Jock, Mary, and Jeff for their hospitality and friendship. To editor Greg McNamee, special thanks for your talented wordsmithing and challenging questions. And to Pam, as always.

Lastly, I extend my gratitude to the people and organizations working to preserve and enhance the special qualities that make their community special. You know who you are. Think about this tourism thing.

*D.S. Phoenix*
*August 2007*